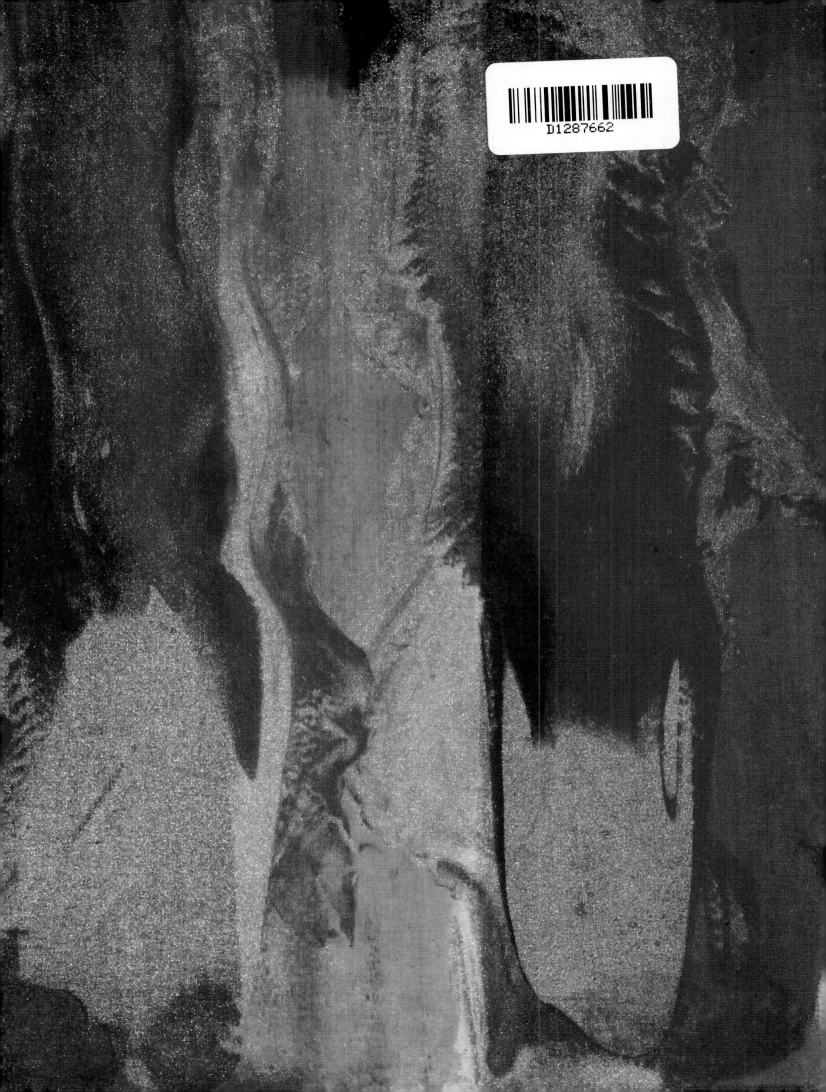

TEXTILE PRINTING

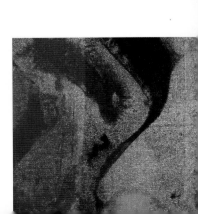

TEXTILE PRINTING

TEXTILE PRINTING

Text:
Eva Pascual I Miró and the chapter titled "A Brief History Of Textile Printing" written by M. Teresa Canals I Aromi.

Exercises:
Miriam Albiñana, Rosa Oliveras, Joan Albert Sánchez, and Elisa Rubio, with the collaboration of Rosa M. Martín on "Color."

Photography:
Nos & Soto, M. Teresa Canals (History), and Sergi Oriola (page 65).

Drawings:
Jaume Farrés

Original title of the book in Spanish: Estampación
© Copyright Parramón Ediciones, S.A., – World Rights
Published by Parramón ediciones, S.A., Barcelona, Spain.

Translated from the Spanish by Michael Brunelle and Beatriz Cortabarria.

First edition for the United States, its territories and possessions, and Canada, published in 2012 by Barron's Educational Series, Inc.

English ed: © 2012 by Barron's Educational Series, Inc.

All inquiries should be addressed to:
Barron's Educational Series, Inc.
250 Wireless Boulevard
Hauppauge, New York, 11788
www.barronseduc.com

ISBN: 978-0-7641-6472-9

Library of Congress Control Number: 2011027526

Library of Congress Cataloging-in-Publication Data
Estampación. English.
  Textile printing / [translated from the Spanish by Michael Brunelle and Beatriz Cortabarria]. — English language ed.
    p. c.m.
  Originally published: Barcelona, Spain : Parramón ediciones.
  Includes bibilographical references.
  ISBN 978-0-7641-6472-9
  1. Textile printing.   I. Barron's Educational Series, Inc.   I. Title.
TT852.E8813   2012
746.6'2—dc23   2011027526

Printed in China
9 8 7 6 5 4 3 2 1

Con

ents

Introduction

The evolution of printing has paralleled that of textiles, and both of them have paralleled the history of mankind. Thus, textiles and the decoration printed on them are a reflection of the material possibilities of the places where they were produced, and of the technical advances resulting from each cultural moment. Research on new textile materials and new printing techniques were carried out at the same time that innovations were applied to the processes, and this happened especially during the second half of the nineteenth century. Nowadays, the techniques and processes of industrial printing are constantly evolving to satisfy the growing demands of business. The development of new fibers and creative designs based on computer technology has opened up a wide range of possibilities. Moreover, the interest in environmental issues, which has encouraged the manufacture of materials (especially dyes and paints, but also fibers) that are respectful of the environment and also of people.

The printing of textiles approached as an artistic discipline offers interesting opportunities for expression. In this book, written as a practical manual, you will find detailed information about the history of textile printing and the most common fabrics used, as well as the basic fundamentals of printing on textiles in the studio. It is explained in a simple and enjoyable, yet precise, manner. The technical processes are carefully explained and include examples to make them easier to understand.

This book is divided into five large chapters. The first relates a brief history of textile printing. The second chapter explains fibers in detail and the characteristics of fabrics, showing a wide-ranging view of those that are used the most. The third chapter talks about the materials and tools used in the different techniques, and they are grouped according to their use, with advice on safety whenever it may be necessary and with recommendations of things to keep in mind in the studio. In the fourth chapter the processes of the basic techniques of textile printing are explained in full detail, grouped by technical type; there is a section on printing techniques, including block printing, serigraphy, bleaching and devoré, and another section on the reserve techniques, which includes batik and serti. We have not tried to completely cover all the techniques, since that would exceed the scope of this work. Here, we compile the basics of this artistic discipline that are required for doing work in the studio.

In every case we offer methods and approaches for carrying out any process successfully. We have attempted to present a unique point of view, with examples where the creative components are emphasized as references. Finally, in the step-by-step chapter, there are six projects explained very carefully, and the entire creative process is explained in detail. These exercises are presented as suggestions from a creative point of view, and this is also reflected in the examples of different artists who illustrate the techniques and in the interesting gallery at the end. A glossary with definitions of the main concepts and a bibliography serve as references for those wishing to delve further into the subject.

This book is not a definitive manual on textile printing; it is just an attempt to present a clear and complete vision from a creative point of view of an activity that requires constant research. We encourage those who have this book in hand to learn about the art that the authors are passionate about, and to investigate it and experiment with creating unique works in your own personal language.

Miriam Albiñana Trias graduated from a program in design and plastic arts, specializing in textile printing, from l'Escola Superior de Disseny i d'Art Llotja, where she held the position of Coordinator in the Department of Textile Printing and Dying. She has coordinated numerous exhibits on textile printing and is a specialist in trends and a coordinator of a specialized international magazine about printing trends called *Texitura*.

Rosa Oliveras has a degree in fine arts from the Universidad de Barcelona with a specialty in painting. She has had several individual shows and is a professor of Artistic Drawing and Color at l'Escola superior de Disenny i d'Art Llotja. She is also a contributor to the magazine *Texitura*.

Eva Pascual i Miró has a degree in art history from the Universidad de Barcelona and specialties in museography, design, and restoration from the Universidad Politécnica de Catalunya. She has done research on medieval Catalan furniture. She is the coauthor of the books *Restoring Wood*, *Stained Glass*, and *Leather*.

Joan Albert Sánchez Sánchez has a degree in fine arts from the Universidad de Barcelona with a specialty in painting, and he has done graduate work in textile printing at l'Escola Superior de Disseny i d'Art Llotja. He also has a studio master's degree in textile design. He is a contributor to the magazine *Texitura*.

Elisa Rubió Ferrer has a degree in fine arts from l'Escola Sant Jordi, Universidad de Barcelona. She has participated in numerous individual and group exhibitions and has been shown in the Museum of Modern Art in Paris. She has been a professor of printed textile design at l'Escola Superior de Disseny i d'Art Llotja. She is a contributor to the magazine *Texitura*.

*F*rom antiquity, people have been taking advantage of the wide range of coloring agents available in nature to change the way blouses, suits, and dresses looked, by making them different colors. By looking at the decorative elements used in clothing we can study the art that went into the textile printing process. Throughout history, the secret of color and how to obtain it has been a preoccupation not only for dyers and colorists but also for scientists. Isaac Newton (1642–1727) studied and wrote in his work *Opticks* on the subject of the disassembly of white light into different colors, namely red, yellow, and blue. His research became the basis for continuous experiments that culminated in the discovery of artificial coloring agents in the nineteenth century, which freed textile printers from their dependence on harvests and imported dyeing material. Over the years, the development of science and the applications from chemical industries—and technology in particular—has made different textile printing methods possible. This has allowed the reproduction of many beautiful designs, which have been created from an infinite range of synthetic colors. However, in the twenty-first century we can still find small groups and individual artisans that use the old textile techniques of dyeing with natural colors, using manual printing, the spinning wheel and spindle, and the low warp loom. In some way, perhaps unconsciously, they are the ones who pass down a cultural heritage that teaches us to use the products provided by nature— transforming them, but without harming them.

A Brief History of
Textile Printing

Textile Printing: Art, Craft, and Technique

When we think or talk about prints, the first thing that comes to mind is mainly a series of multicolor dresses, or curtains and upholstered furniture. We often forget that the printing of images on materials other than textiles has been practiced since antiquity, although they used different approaches and different materials than the ones we use today.

Background (A World Without Printed Images)

The printing process consists of transferring an image from a matrix or block to the chosen support. Roman ambassadors and consuls, for example, used their seals as stamps, which had previously been carved on a signet ring in accordance with their assigned rank and power.

Different printing systems were also used on ceramic and glass objects, but especially on leather. Wood block prints on paper, as well as printed copper plates, have produced very high-quality reproductions since the twelfth century and have enjoyed great prestige, to the point that well-known artists from different periods (A. Dürer, Rembrandt, F. de Goya, P. Picasso, J. Miró, and others) made reproductions of their work using this method that have come to us in the form of numbered art prints. We can perfectly adapt the technique of wood block printing (as well as serigraphy and lithography) to textile printing, especially the first phases of the manual process, which continue to be employed in certain non-industrialized areas of Asia and Africa.

Textile printing in old Europe, the knowledge of which was exported to America as well, is a process that has been applied to and is practiced in the modern era, which is barely three hundred years old. This is strange because leaving a trace or mark on something is a very old practice. What has been researched for centuries is the way to preserve such marks.

Printing a design on a surface made of textile fibers seems easy, and in fact it is. Pieces of Egyptian tunics from the fifth and sixth centuries of our era have been found adorned with biblical scenes that could have been printed with a technique similar to batik. However, if we expect them to withstand daily wear and tear, exposure to air and sun, and washing, then it is necessary for the fabric to first be properly treated with mordants, and then for the dye to be mixed with the appropriate thickeners and additives for application to the raw material, whatever it may be.

The Art of Dyeing

Humans have always used the things that nature had to offer them, and they have transformed these things and adapted them to their needs. So, obtaining dyes from natural sources (animal, vegetable, and mineral) is something that dates back to prehistoric times. Specifically, humans have found pieces of fabric colored with blue dye extracted from the leaves of the pastel plant, from the Neolithic period, as well as from the yellow dye that comes from a plant called weld (or dyer's weed). Later, a precious purple color, an extract from the Murex snail, was discovered and used by the Phoenicians, and a few centuries later the color became a symbol of distinction for senators and emperors from the Roman Empire.

◀ Original drawing for textile printing from the *indianas* factories in Barcelona, Spain. Latter part of the eighteenth century. Santiago Moreno collection, slide 31. AHC (Arxiu Històric de la Ciutat. Institut de Cultura de Barcelona), Barcelona, Spain.

▲ *Indiana* fragment. Cotton fabric printed by hand. Design based on flora and fauna from Asia. From the western area of India. 32 × 44 inches (82 × 112 cm). Produced between 1675 and 1700. Conseil Régional de la Reunion. Musée des Arts Décoratifs de l'Océan Indien. Inventory number: Tex.: 003.1764.

The use, application, and study of dyes developed uninterruptedly, and they were increasingly important, as the demand for dyed wool, silk, and linen increased. Because of its complexity, knowledge of science and dyeing substances was required. Over the centuries, this became a matter of state, to such an extent that in Spain and in France during the seventeenth and eighteenth centuries the position of Director and Inspector of the Kingdom's Dye Trade was established. The person who had this position was in charge of inspecting everything that was related to the manufacturing of this product, knowing and controlling all the land cultivated with dye plants like madder, and additionally, writing specific treaties on the subject. One of the best known is, without a doubt, the *Tratado instructivo y práctico sobre el arte de la tintura* (Instructional and Practical Treaty On The Art of Dyeing) by Luis Fernández (Madrid, 1778).

In the seventeenth and eighteenth centuries, excellent results were achieved in the dyeing of fabrics for upholstery and clothing; however, in Europe there was neither a system nor the knowledge of how to transfer a design onto fabric—in other words, how to print with solid colors. Ornamentation consisted mainly of embroideries on rich velvet and silk fabrics and of sumptuous damasks and brocades whose drawings were woven in with a combination of gold and silver threads. However, these materials were only available to the wealthy.

The reasons that inhibited the development of a printing method were many, but they were mainly related to the lack of scientific knowledge with respect to the use and application of dyes on textiles—that is, to the field that is known today as chemistry. Also, there were many circumstances (in this case, international) that helped make the creation of the printing trade possible.

The Dyeing Materials That Came from the Orient

During the sixteenth, seventeenth, and eightennth centuries, the new territories discovered by Europeans began to be slowly and arduously explored, and newly discovered raw materials, manufacturing products, and indigenous traditions started to be exchanged with those of the old continent.

The new maritime routes initiated by the Portuguese, who were in search of the most valued spices, motivated the most daring to sail the Asian seas. As a result, pearls, ivory, and porcelain, as well as objects made of shell, coral, and jade came out of China and India, and multicolor printed fabrics (painted with a brush) representing the flora and fauna of those countries started to arrive as well. A printing method using wax reserves

▲ *Cornucopia.* Hand-printed cotton scarf for the European market. India (Coromandel Coast). 22 × 22 inches (55.5 × 55.5 cm). Circa 1780. Conseil Régional de la Reunion. Musée des Arts Décoratifs de l'Océan Indien. Inventory number: Tex.: 004.1785.

and its production, which is known as batik, came from the island of Java. The designs reproduced on cloth were fascinating, but the most important thing in the eyes of European manufacturers was the solidity of their colors, of which some tones were unknown up to that point.

The arrival of those goods marked the beginning of a new industry. On the one hand, they started to import dyeing materials; on the other, trying to replicate the new tones required arduous research that was shared equally by small local studios and large manufacturing companies located in sections that were beginning to define Europe's future industrialized areas.

It was of utmost importance to obtain, learn about, and discover the ideal components for fixing and stabilizing the color on textile fibers. They turned out to be mainly metal salts, such as ferrous sulfate, copper, and aluminum nitrate, among others. Once the mordants were identified it was discovered that they not only fixed the color but that, in some cases, they had the ability to create new shades of color.

◄ The valued red color is obtained from the root of a plant called madder. When we prepare each of the different natural fibers (cotton, linen, silk, and wool) with the corresponding mordants (ferrous salts), the result is different shades of the color red.

The *Indianas*

Multicolored printed fabrics started to arrive in Europe from the newly discovered territories (mainly from Macao and Canton). It was clear that not only the colors but also the material from which the fabric was made was of great importance. More specifically, it was the source of the fibers, which came mainly from plants—especially from cotton. This plant was already known in Europe (imported from Egypt) and was grown in the southern part of the Iberian Peninsula, but the American material was superior in quality and more plentiful. Despite the distance, it was imported in mass quantities and its production set the basis for large-scale industrialization. It is important to mention that in the same installations where the printing process took place, there were also looms to weave the base material so that both the quality and the source of the cotton could be controlled.

These printed fabrics were referred to as "*indianas*" (coming from India) or "painted." The name became popular and has survived to this day, which is why printed cotton fabrics—mainly the ones with floral themes—are still called *indianas* in Spain (in England they are known as *calicos*, and in France *cotonnades*).

However, when they were beginning to arrive, these printed fabrics were considered a luxury item because of their scarcity and novelty, and considering the added value of their origin—distant unknown lands—they were reserved for the royalty and aristocracy. With time, as a result of the establishment of factories in the main cities (and port areas) for this trade, printed fabric gradually became available to the emerging bourgeoisie. Once the printer's profession was established, anyone could practice it; all that was needed was a long and durable table, blocks with the design, a mallet for tapping the blocks, pigments, glues, ferrous salt, thickeners, and the rest of the products, such as fabric and plenty of water for rinsing and washing. At this point multicolored prints became available to the popular classes and the most humble homes, since cotton, once woven, can be washed and hung to dry in the sun with better results than other types of fibers.

Manufacturers and Merchants

The first shops for printing *indianas* were established in Marseille (an important port for the commerce with America) in the seventeenth century, followed by establishments located in London and Amsterdam, although not much is known about them. The activities related to the manufacturing of this material were not really documented until the last quarter of the eighteenth century. The main areas were Mulhouse, Rouen, and Nantes in France. Also, England, Switzerland, and the southern part of Germany were involved in this type of industry. In Spain, the city of Barcelona was the first to open an establishment of this kind, and by 1768 there were already twenty-two factories dedicated to this trade. By 1784 there were seventy-four *indiana* establishments that produced 7,403,426 yards (6,769,693 meters) of printed fabric per year (Thompson, 1990). In fact, the archives of some of these factories (Fons Gónima.BC) have been preserved, which makes it possible for us to learn about the clients and the orders that they had from all over the country and from Europe, as well as about their exports to La Habana, Veracruz, and Cumaná, among others, during the entire nineteenth century.

Normally, these establishments were located in the old sections of town, inside the city walls and near some type of water source, since abundant water was needed for the multiple rinsing steps (in the textile argot, the workers of this specialty are known as the "water trade").

Women and children, with their small and nimble hands, removed the seeds and other impurities found in the natural plant from the raw fabric. The boys helped prepare the pigments with the corresponding agglutinates and they poured them in *baques*, or containers. The male specialists printed by

▼ Printing table, fabric, wooden block, mallet, *baque*, and container for the colorant. Reproduction of an artisanal printing shop from the first quarter of the nineteenth century. MEP.

▼ Printed indigo blue sample. La España Industrial. Barcelona, 1880. MEP.

▲ *"Indiana"* or *Palampore*. Cotton piece for decorative purposes, painted and printed by hand, from India (Coromandel Coast). Composition based on the symbols from the tree of life. 96.5 × 71.5 inches (245 × 182 cm). First part of the eighteenth century. Conséil Régional de La Reunion. Musée des Arts Décoratifs de l'Océan Indien. Inventory number: Tex.: 991.0744.

striking the wooden blocks with a mallet. Others hung the decorated fabrics to dry. These steps were carried out on a small or large scale, depending on the size of the company.

Vast areas of grassy land were also needed to spread the fabrics that had been bleached and prepared with the required glues before they were ready for color. These lands came to be known as the "*indiana* lands," and they were normally located in the outskirts of the cities, near fields and gardens.

A special board for this particular trade was created in Barcelona in 1758 to control the quality of the product that was to be exported, to prevent contraband, and to keep track of the newly formed factories. They redacted, among other things, the *Ordenanzas de las Fábricas de Indianas* (Bylaws of the Indianas Factories). Also important was the creation in 1775 of the Escuela Gratuita de Diseño (Free School of Design), which was the predecessor of the current Escola de Llotja, whose mission was to prepare drawing and printing specialists for the *indianas*.

▲ Detail from the previous piece.

Designs, Drawings, and Draftsmen: Art at the Service of Industry

Internationally known artists used the printing techniques as a way to make their work available and disseminate it in a different way. We know that before the printing process, it is absolutely necessary to complete certain steps to arrive at the final image. In other words, there are other professions without which it would not be possible to carry out the printing process. One of the most important steps is to choose the desired drawing or image for reproduction. Certain printed pieces can become true works of art. First, a copy or original design that is expressly commissioned for the occasion is selected. Then, the next step is to carve the image onto the block, matrix, or cylinder that will be used for printing.

In the beginning, the profession of a printer who carved on wooden blocks or copper plates required a lot of patience, skill, and knowledge of the entire process, because the chosen drawing had to be broken down according to the number of colors that needed to be printed, since each color requires the use of a different block or cylinder. Also, the dimensions of the drawing had to conform to the tools and machinery that were being used. The factories that were able to carry out the entire process had an advantage because the draftsmen, carvers, printers, and others worked as teams and knew the final product that they were aiming for; therefore, they were able to obtain optimum results.

With regard to the designs on cotton, at the beginning they were copied from the embroideries and brocades that were being produced in silk manufacturing plants, mainly floral designs and related colorful decorative motifs. They consisted of small motifs that were repeated time and time again, which can still be seen on the fabrics that line trunks and trundles, folding screens, parasols, and other items of that time.

► Trunk lined with printed fabric. The items inside are also printed: a roll of printed paper in the *Toile de Jouy* style, a striped skirt, etc. End of the nineteenth century. MEP.

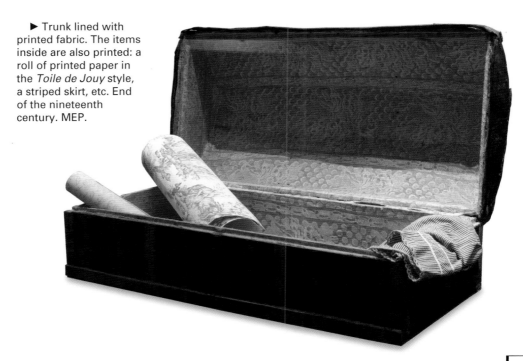

Designers of every period follow the fashion of the time, or they come up with their own creations. However, until the twentieth century they needed to conform to the industry because they had to be aware of the chemical process that was available for producing the printing colors. Also, they needed to know the process involved in the carving of the blocks, and what blocks to avoid (for example, stripes and other vertical motifs were difficult to line up and transfer until the cylinder machines became available). Some of these artists became true experts in motifs for the *indianas* and were often summoned to important factories. They often studied and trained in France and worked in England, or vice versa. Some tapestries still bear the name of the artist, but in general they were not known.

Some twentieth-century artists have occasionally designed exclusive models for high fashion, like the Russian painter Sonia Delaunay, who in 1925 presented her creations based on geometric motifs in pure and luminous colors, making her "art work universal and portable."

In 1948, Henri Matisse elevated the murals printed with motifs from his designs to art status. Today, they can be seen in museums in the United States.

▶ *Kalamkar*. Cotton fabric dyed, printed, and painted by hand from India or Persia. Dimensions 67 × 77 inches (170 × 196 cm). Beginning of the twentieth century. Decorative motifs based on Islamic symbols centered on a cypress tree (the symbol of eternity), finished with a multi-oval arch that evokes the door to paradise. Conseil Régional de la Reunion. Musée des Arts Décoratifs de l'Océan Indien. Inventory number: Tex.: 991.0749.

Also, the multifaceted painter Salvador Dalí created exclusive designs that became printed dresses for his wife, Gala, some of which are displayed in the Púbol Castle (Girona).

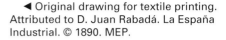

◀ Original drawing for textile printing. Attributed to D. Juan Rabadá. La España Industrial. © 1890. MEP.

Industrialization. The New Discoveries in Chemistry

Discoveries in the field of chemistry changed the appearance of prints. Different additions, inventions, and novelties improved the quality of the products and freed the manufacturers from constant trial and error processes.

Michel-Eugène Chevreul (1786–1889) was the director of the French tapestry manufacturer Gobelins, and he specialized in dyeing. His studies were focused on color contrasts, and he realized that light is the origin of color and that it is important to differentiate between primary colors (blue, red, and yellow) and secondary colors (mixtures of the former). His discoveries, which he left us on his magnus opum: *De la loi du contraste simultané des couleurs* (*The Principles of Harmony and Contrast of Colors*), set the stage for all the color research of the nineteenth century.

◀ Four-panel folding screen in printed cotton fabric. Barcleona, circa 1900. CDMT (Centre de documentació i Museu Textil) Terrassa (Spain) 18168. © CDMT (Quico Ortega).

In 1856, the young Englishman W. Perkin revolutionized the dye and printing industries by synthesizing the first mauve or violet aniline dye in his laboratory from coal tar.

These discoveries represented the culmination of two centuries of study and, in some way, the beginning of the end of an artisanal culture based on recipes and mechanical processes of old factories passed down orally. It was time to make way for the new chemical processes and the modern textile factories. Although natural dyes coexisted with artificial pigments for years, beginning in the last third of the nineteenth century the fledgling chemical industries of southern Germany and Switzerland manufactured and commercialized the new aniline dyes, whose use expanded rapidly, lessening the use of natural anilines, campeche wood, and cochineal from the colonies and practically abandoning them completely.

▲ Wool dress dyed in bright violet color thanks to the artificial dyes that emerged in the second half of the nineteenth century. Designs printed by hand with wood blocks. Rich designs inspired by Kashmir leaves. French-made (Mulhouse), circa 1865. Musée de l'impression sur étoffes. Mulhouse (France). Inventory number: 999-58.1.

Machines and the New Technology

Since the latter part of the eighteenth century, different mechanical printing tests were conducted using machines with wood or copper cylinders, with the design for each color carved on individual cylinders, which replaced the slow manual process.

The United Kingdom was a pioneer in the mechanization of the textile industry, and despite the registered trademarks, there was a certain amount of "industrial espionage" between the different European countries who wanted to copy and develop the new machinery. The new systems made mass production—thousands of printed yards—possible. They have lasted until the middle of the twentieth century, with the obvious technological changes, which were naturally in competition with other methods.

At the beginning of the twentieth century, the old silk screen–printing technique from Japan, also known as "*à la Lyonnaise*" (after the French city of Lyon, where they specialized in this system) was recovered and reinstated. Also during the early years of the last century, the first factory was established in Spain, with French money, in the city of Premià de Mar (Barcelona), which was called Lyon-Barcelona. This type of printing and its large "screens" made of transparent mesh made it possible—and still does—to print large pieces of fabric, like bed sheets.

During the second half of the twentieth century, especially during the 1970s, a new revolution took place, which began with the introduction of the rotating printing system "*à la Lyonnaise*." Cylinders are carved with a computer program that uses plotters to etch the drawing on nickel plates.

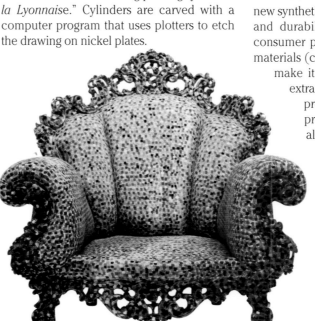

▶ *Poltrona de Proust*, designed by Alessandro Mendini for Studio Alchimia. Printed by hand with acrylic paint, including the wood structure. Milan, 1978.

▲ Cotton fabric printed with a design by J. Vila Grau, 1964, which received the FAD.MEP Award.

Obviously, the creation and transfer of art has also changed and evolved, since scanning an original design makes color breakdown much simpler: it makes it possible to adapt to the dimensions very quickly and also allows the colors to be tested on paper, letting us preview the final result.

Little by little, computer technology is being integrated, which, in a short amount of time—and perhaps only for small quantities—can print the design directly from the printer.

Nowadays, most of the textile industries follow the guidelines stipulated by the European Union in terms of pollutants and their impact on the environment; that is, they only use dyes that do not harm the environment.

Paradoxically, and after having discovered new synthetic fibers that offer more resistance and durability (and are more affordable), consumer preference tends to favor natural materials (cotton, linen). New advances also make it possible to incorporate natural extracts that have health benefits (they prevent allergies, have anti-stress properties, etc.), like chamomile, aloe vera, and ginseng.

M. Teresa Canals Aromí
Director of the Museu de l'Estampació de Premià de Mar, Barcelona.

Textiles for Printing

*I*n this chapter we present in detail the main fabrics that can be used for printed works. You will see that knowledge of textiles is fundamental, since the process of printing, the chosen technique, and the final result will be directly affected by the material, that is, the fabric. It is very important to choose fabric based on the project and the technique you wish to employ. In the first part we explain the different fibers according to where they come from, show the most typical ones with their main characteristics and properties, and give a series of guidelines for identifying them. Then, the main structures of the fabrics are explained in complete detail. Finally, we show a wide range of common textiles made of natural and artificial fibers, and we explain the characteristics that are used to identify them.

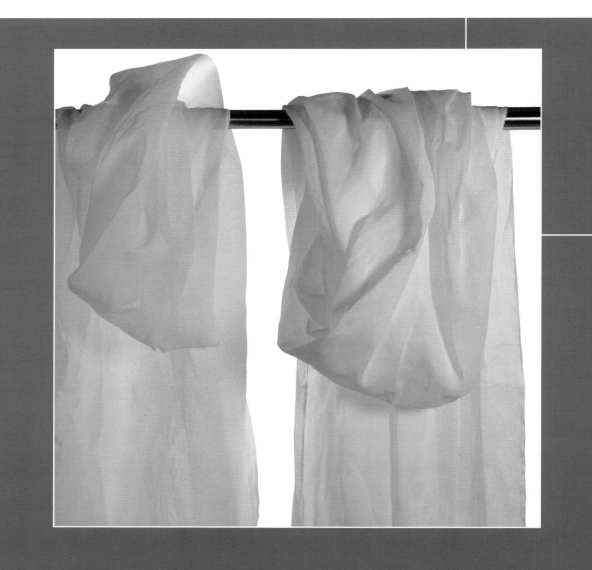

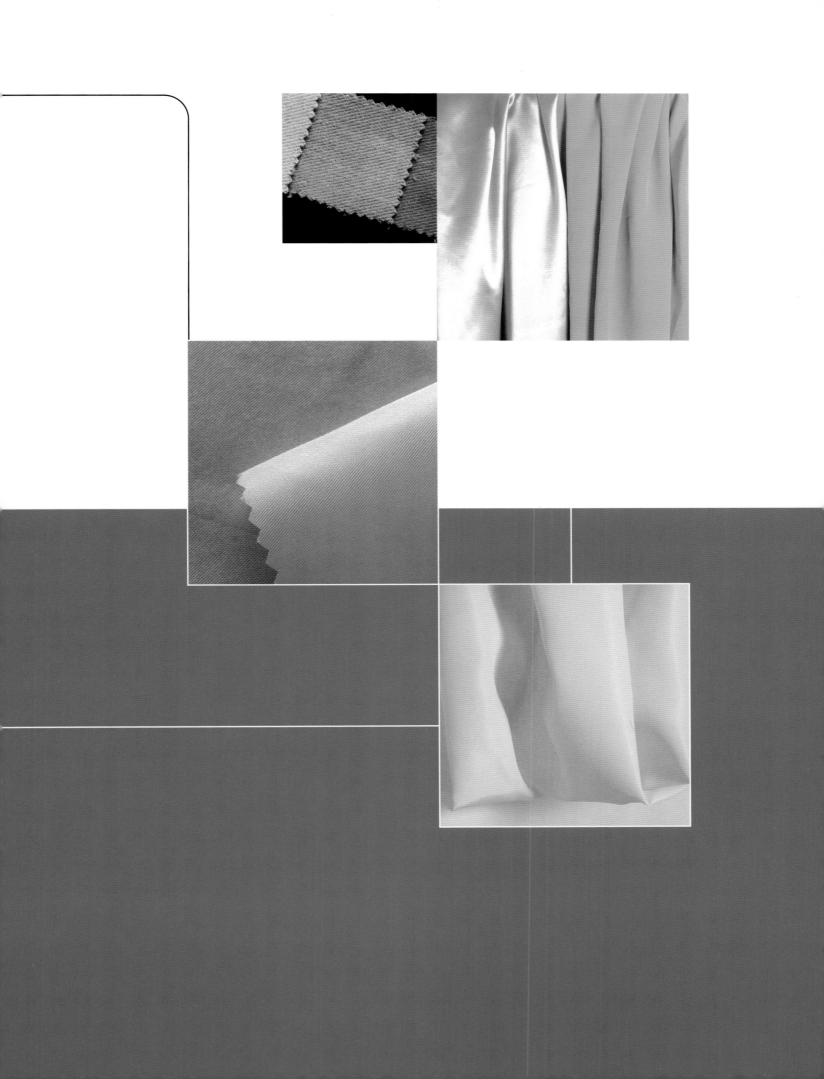

Fibers

Textiles are woven fabrics made from textile fibers, that is, they are flat structures made by weaving a series of fibers. The fibers are composed of many filaments that form long and thin threads, which are used to weave the fabric. These fibers are the raw materials of textiles, and they determine their basic characteristics. The fibers used for making textiles can be natural or artificial.

Natural Fibers

Natural fibers can be of vegetable origin (linen, cotton, hemp, etc.) or animal (mainly silk and wool), although there are also fibers of mineral origin, such as asbestos.

Vegetable fibers come from plants and are composed in large part of cellulose, a polymer of glucose molecules. Cellulose is a very chemically stable molecule and is not water-soluble; it is hygroscopic (absorbs water and swells), decomposes in the presence of acids, and decomposes for various reasons. These are what determine the characteristics of cellulosic and vegetable fibers. Fibers of animal origin come from the hair of some mammals or filaments secreted by a particular insect, composed of proteins—macromolecules formed by chains of amino acids. These fibrous proteins have long chains, are not soluble in water or wet solutions, and add strength and durability to the hair or filament.

Next we will point out the principal natural fibers used for manufacturing textiles.

Cotton

The cotton plant is bushy and herbaceous and can grow to 3 to 6 feet (1 to 2 meters) in height. It belongs to the genus *gossipium*. The cotton itself is the fiber that covers the seed of the plant. Depending on the species of plant, cotton fiber differs in color, sheen, feel, elasticity, and size. A great proportion of cotton is cellulose, and it is very hygroscopic; in the presence of excessive humidity it reacts very quickly: the fibers swell and later shrink, causing mechanical forces of contraction. It is durable, resistant to both moths and acids, and very flammable.

Linen

Linen (*linum usitatissimum vulgare*) is a plant with a fibrous bark and bluish flowers. The textile fibers, which are obtained by macerating the fibers of the stem of the plant, measure from 2.5 to 23.5 inches (6 to 60 cm) long and from 0.0005 to 0.001 inches (0.012 to 0.026 mm) wide. They are nearly pure cellulose, although they also have some lignin (a compound that forms part of the cellular walls of plants), which gives them a brownish tone. Linen fibers are stronger than cotton fibers and are very fine, but they are not very elastic or flexible. The seeds are used to manufacture linseed oil.

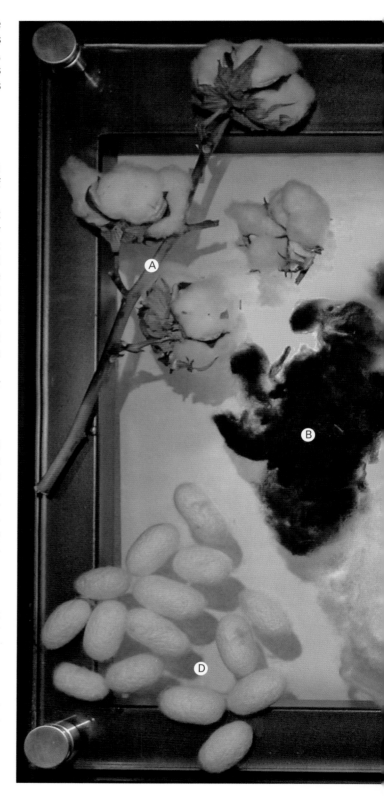

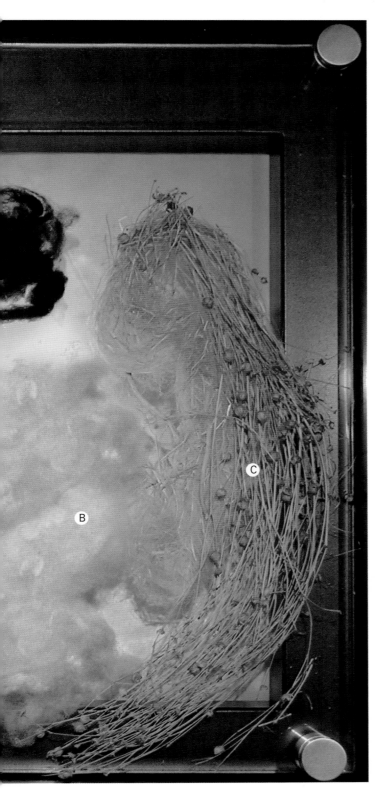

Other Vegetable Fibers

There are other vegetable fibers that are used for making textiles, among them hemp, jute, sisal, and ramie. Hemp (*cannabis sativa*) is a plant from the cannabinaceae family. Its textile fibers are obtained just like those of linen, by macerating the stem of the plant. These are very solid and tenacious fibers, and they are shiny with colors that run from light to very dark yellow. Hemp does not look as fine as linen, but it is stronger and longer lasting than cotton. Jute (*Corchorua olitorius* and *Corchorus capsulares*) is a bush from the malvaceae family that is cultivated in tropical regions for its fibers. It is the most widely used fiber after cotton, it has a high lignin content, and it is cheap and easy to weave, although it deteriorates easily. Ramie (*Boehmeria nivea*) is a perennial plant, and the fibers are extracted from its stem. The fibers of the ramie are white and silky; they are the most durable of known fibers and among the longest of the plant kingdom, although they are difficult to extract.

Wool

Wool is the hair of some species of animals, and after it is shorn, washed, dried, degreased, bleached, dyed, carded, and spun, it is used as a fiber to manufacture textiles. It is obtained mainly from domestic sheep, but it can also come from other animals: camels, alpacas, llamas, vicuñas, different species of goats, etc. Wool fibers are composed mainly of keratin proteins. They are very elastic (they can stretch about 50 percent of their length without breaking) and fine, but they are not very durable. They are the most hygroscopic of those used for weaving fabrics. Wool fibers are heat sensitive, and they vary from 20 to 25 microns in diameter to 2 to 6 inches (55 to 150 mm) in length.

Silk

Silk is a product of saliva, which solidifies when it comes into contact with the air. It is made by the silkworm (*Bombix mori*) to create the cocoon in which it will complete its metamorphosis. From the cocoon are obtained filaments from 15 to 60 inches (38 to 152 cm) long. Silk thread is composed of a protein (fibroin) in the form of filaments joined by sericin, another protein that is eliminated by heating. Silk is a very strong material and is easy to dye, but it breaks down over time. It is also susceptible to attacks by insects and microorganisms and is extremely sensitive to light. It decomposes at 338°F (170°C).

◄ Cotton branch (A), wool (B), linen (C), and silk cocoons (D). Photograph of a display in the Museu de l'Estampació de Premiá de Mar, Barcelona.

Artificial Fibers

Artificial fibers are fibers that have been manufactured in some way. They can be regenerated fibers, manufactured from the transformation of natural polymers like cellulose, or synthetic fibers, manufactured from polymers made by industry with mainly petroleum derivatives.

Regenerated Fibers

One of the first artificial fibers ever made was rayon, also known as viscose rayon, which was developed from cellulose treated with an alkali. It is a very versatile fiber that is used to imitate the look and feel of some natural fibers such as silk and cotton. It is very absorbent and is the least elastic of all the textile fibers. Cellulose acetate, also known as rayon acetate, was developed from cotton and woods rich in cellulose (a natural polymer) that decompose in acetic sulphuric acid. The fibers of cellulose acetate are thermoplastic, that is, when they are given a determined form under heat they maintain it. They are hydrophilic—meaning they absorb water easily—hypoallergenic, and resistant to mold, but they will dissolve in most solvents. It is a fiber appreciated for its use in the manufacture of textiles, its low cost of manufacture, and its low impact on the environment since it is made from renewable resources like those obtained from sustainable plants and can be recycled.

Acrylic

Acrylic fibers are produced from a chemical compound (acrylic acid) that comes from propylene, a gaseous byproduct of refined petroleum. Acrylic acid tends to create polymers, which, once neutralized, are used for the production of fibers, among other applications. Acrylic fibers are used to imitate the look of wool. They are very light and elastic, and they are resistant to insect attacks, oils, chemical products, and sunlight.

Polyester

Polyester fiber (polyethylene terephthalate polymers) is the most widely used synthetic fiber. It is combined with other fibers such as cotton, linen, and wool to create textiles. The characteristics of these fibers depend on their chemical composition, but they are generally very strong and elastic, and resistant to light and solvents. They absorb less moisture than acrylic fibers.

Polyamide

Polyamides, originally know as nylon, are polymers that have monomers of amides joined by peptide bonds. They make excellent fibers because they form regular symmetrical chains, with the amides groups attached to each other to create a crystalline structure. They melt at 128°F (263°C). These fibers are very resistant to tension, tearing, abrasion, and bending, as well as solvents, but they are not acid resistant. Just like polyester fibers they maintain their elasticity in the cold, that is, they can be stretched to several times their length without being warmed up. Today there are many polyamide fibers; the most common is nylon, of which there are several different kinds.

▼ The structure of nylon 6 and nylon 6.6.

NYLON 6

NYLON 6.6

⬤ NITROGEN　⬤ CARBON　⬤ OXYGEN　◯ HYDROGEN

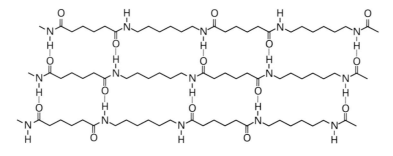

► In nylon the amide groups bond to each other and allow the polymer chains to align and form fibers.

IDENTIFYING THE FIBERS

In order to correctly identify the fibers that a fabric is made of, first observe its general appearance by looking at and touching it. If there are any doubts about the nature of the fibers, look at them under a microscope and test them by burning.

Observing Fibers Under a Microscope

Cotton	This has a characteristic look that will leave no doubts, because it looks like a band with thick twisted edges, with a channel in the middle.
Linen	Linen fibers have nodules spaced at intervals.
Hemp	These fibers appear in groups and are cylindrical, with transverse partitions and flat ends.
Wool	Wool fibers have characteristic scales, typical of the hair of mammals.
Silk	Treated fibers, heated and without sericin, are easily identified when seen under a microscope, because they have pairs of very fine cylindrical filaments.

Burn Test

This is a very useful method, and although it requires practice and previous knowledge to be able to accurately identify the fiber, those with no experience can determine, by elimination, the origins of the different fibers.

It is done by separating a fiber from the fabric and holding it with tweezers, with a long handle if possible. The test should be done in a safe place, over a large container with water (a sink or a bucket, for example); be very careful to avoid touching your skin or clothing with the burning fiber. Some synthetic fibers melt and create residues that drip and can adhere to the skin and clothing, causing painful burns. To identify the fiber, observe the way it burns, the flame and smoke, and the residue and odor it gives off.

NATURAL FIBERS		Type Of Ignition	Residues
Vegetable	Cotton	Burns quickly, with a steady yellow flame, and causes grayish smoke with the odor of burnt paper.	If you blow on it during the burning, small particles may be released, similar to those seen when blowing out a candle. The residue is ash.
	Linen	Burns quickly, but less than cotton, with a steady yellow flame and grayish smoke with the odor of burnt paper. It is quickly extinguished by blowing on it.	The residue of linen is ash. The area of the fiber near them is extremely fragile.
Animal	Wool	Burns quickly, but less than silk, and is difficult to keep it ignited. The flame is less irregular than that of silk and it emits grayish smoke with the odor of burnt hair.	Very brittle ashes.
	Silk	Burns quickly with an irregular flame that occasionally sparks, emitting grayish smoke with the odor of burnt hair.	Very brittle ashes.
ARTIFICIAL FIBERS		Type Of Ignition	Residues
Regenerated	Cellulose acetate	Burns quickly with a yellowish dancing flame that is not easy to extinguish, emitting grayish smoke with the odor of burning sawdust.	Melts in somewhat hard, small drops of a blackish color.
	Rayon	Burns quickly with a steady yellowish flame, causing grayish smoke with the odor of burnt paper.	Leaves a small residue of fine, light gray–colored ash.
Acrylic		Burns quickly with a very hot bright flame, giving off black smoke with a disagreeable acrid smoke.	Melts in small, hard black drops.
Polyamide		Melts and burns quickly if the flame is held to the melted fiber, and smells of burnt plastic. Displays a yellow flame and gives off gray smoke.	Melts in small, brown, indestructible drops.
Polyester		Melts and burns quickly, with a yellow flame, giving off a blackish smoke with a sweet odor. The melted particles drip, so extra precautions should be taken.	Melts in small, hard drops that are brown and indestructible.

Fabrics

The Structure of Fabrics

Fabrics are made of interwoven threads made of fibers, and the type of fabric is defined by the system of weaving and the kind of thread that is used. Depending on their structure, they can be classified as flat woven fabrics, knit fabrics, and nonwoven fabrics.

Flat Woven Fabrics

Flat woven fabrics are made by constructing or weaving a series of longitudinal threads with another group of perpendicular ones, in other words, the weft and the warp. The warp is the group of threads that are attached to the loom—they are parallel to each other—while the threads of the weft are passed through them, weaving the fabric. They are arranged longitudinally in the fabric and constitute the height of the textile. The weft is made of the threads that are woven through the warp in the direction of the width of the textile. The crossing or weaving of the warp and the weft is called a pass. The width of the textile is determined by the distance between the warp threads on each side, which in turn are defined by the width of the loom itself. The system used for arranging the warp and weft—the way they cross each other—is known as the weave. Every possible manner of combining the passes of the weft through the warp (the weave) can be described, and

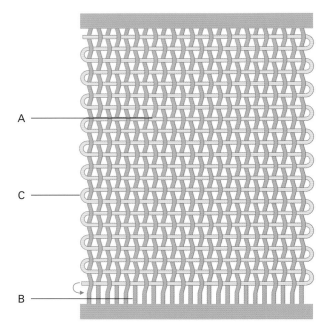

◀ A diagram of the structure of a flat woven or simple weave fabric: weft (A), warp (B), and selvedge (C).

each fabric is defined by the weave. Thus, you can find fabrics with a simple structure formed by the warp and the weft, called the plain weave. There are fabrics woven with two warps and one weft, or two wefts and one warp, and others that use other multiples in their weaving pattern. The following is a list of the most common weaves.

• **Taffeta.** Taffeta is the simplest of the weaves. Each thread of the warp crosses each thread of the weft in an over-under pattern. This weave creates fabrics that do not have a front or back. These textiles are easily identified by the perpendicular structure of the threads.

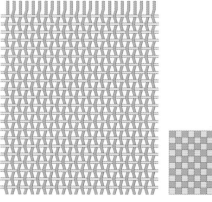

▲ Diagram of the weave of a taffeta fabric.

◀ Taffeta.

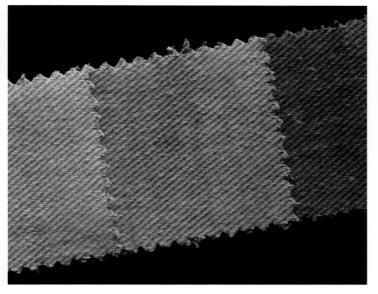

▲ Twill.

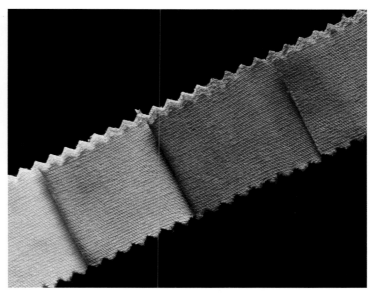

▲ Knit.

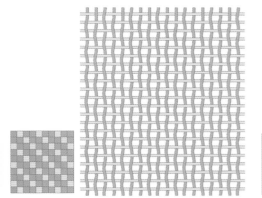

▲ Diagram of the weave of a twill fabric.

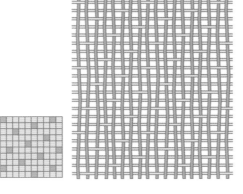

▲ Diagram of the weave of a satin fabric.

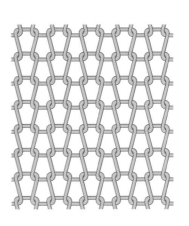

▲ Diagram of a knit fabric.

• **Twill.** In this weave the crossing of the threads moves one space to the side with each pass of the thread of the weft, resulting in a fabric with a diagonal "pattern." The fabric has a front and back. This fabric is easily identified because the surface has lines running at a 45 degree angle. This woven pattern gives the fabric great strength.

• **Satin.** This fabric has a minimal number of crossing threads. They are separated and equidistant from each other, and the threads are not always interwoven, with the weft passing over more than one thread of the warp in a way that makes the weaving invisible. The result is a smooth and very shiny surface. This fabric has a front and back.

Knit Fabric

Knit fabrics are made of a woven mesh. They can be woven on a loom and formed with a single thread that loops through itself, which can break and cause the fabric to come apart. They can also be woven on a warp to make a mesh that cannot unravel, although this method is less common.

Nonwoven Fabrics

Nonwoven fabrics are made with threads, which, joined in a haphazard manner through a special manufacturing process, form a cloth that looks woven but does not have the same structure as woven fabrics. This manufacturing process gives the fabric special resistant characteristics. An example of this type of fabric is felt.

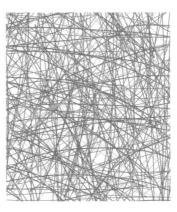

▲ Structure of nonwoven fabrics.

Types of Fabrics

There is an enormous number of fabrics with different structures and weaves, and the names of them vary according to the cultural context and where they are made. Here, we will present the most common ones and the ones most frequently used for printing.

Cambric or Chambray

Cambric is a very fine cotton, cotton polyester, or linen plain weave fabric. The name comes from the hometown of the first manufacturer of this kind of cloth, the weaver Frances Baptiste, who lived in Cambrai, France in the thirteenth century. It is mainly used for the making of shirts, dresses, scarves, and curtains.

Shantung

Originally this was a silk fabric produced in Shantung, China. Nowadays, shantung, sometimes called raw silk, is a plain weave fabric made of wild silk that has a nubby texture. This irregular surface gives it a characteristic rustic look. The wild silk is made from fragmented threads, like those that come from cocoons where the butterfly has emerged after its metamorphosis, and from other discarded silk threads.

◄ Shantung.

▼ Fabrics of cotton (A), linen (B), and wool (C).

A

B

C

Chiffon

This is a French word for a very fine and light fabric that is delicate and sheer but strong, with a slightly rough feel. It is a plain woven cloth made with twisted threads. It can be made of cotton, silk, or artificial fibers like rayon, polyester, and nylon, although it is usually associated with silk or nylon. It is used for making lingerie, blouses, and ribbons.

Crape

This is an English version of the French *crêpe*, which means curly or twisted, and refers to certain fabrics made of wool, cotton, silk, or artificial fabrics that have a rough surface. Thin crape is also called *crêpe de Chine*. It is a plain woven cloth in which the threads of the warp are more twisted than those of the weft, giving it a wavy look. Silk crape is a fine fabric with a matte look with a rough texture. It is used for dresses, blouses, and shirts.

▲ Silk chiffon.

▼ Fabrics of silk (A), artificial cloth (B), and a mixture of artificial fibers with cotton (C).

A

B

C

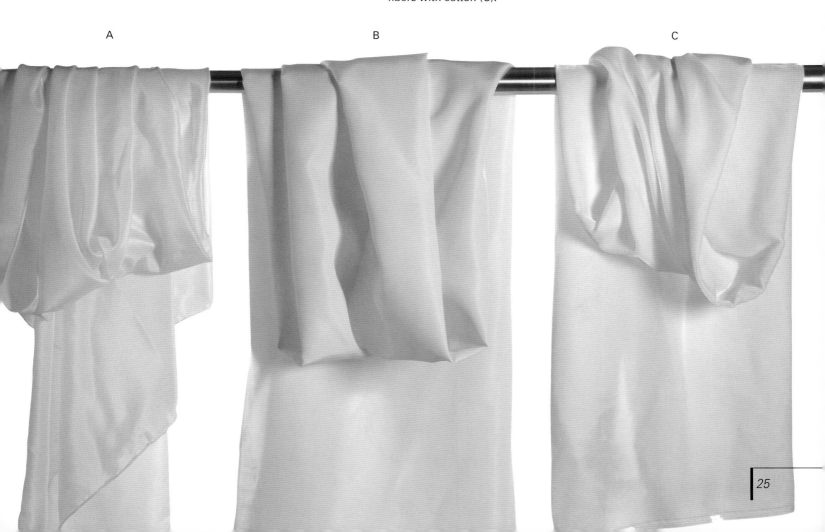

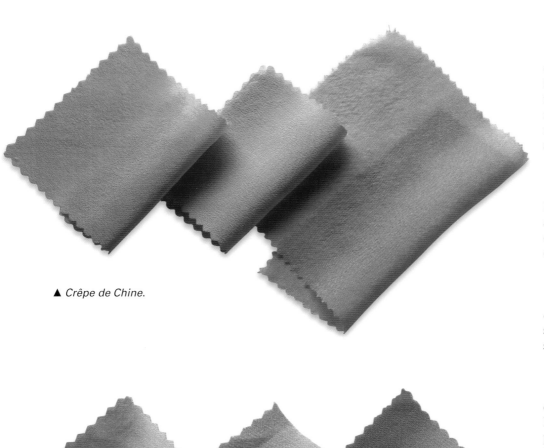

▲ *Crêpe de Chine.*

Crêpe de Chine

Crêpe de Chine is a silk cloth that has characteristics similar to those of crape, but it is somewhat lighter and softer, with less texture and not as much marked relief. It does not wrinkle very much, and it is used for making dress clothes, decorations, and accessories.

Georgette

Shortened from *crêpe georgette*, this is a light and elastic crape that drapes well, is soft and has a dull finish, and is stronger than chiffon. It is mainly used for making dress clothing.

Satin Crape

Satin crape, sometimes known as *angel crape*, is a very densely woven cloth that is soft and reversible, with one side having a satiny sheen and the other dull and rough.

Gauze

This name comes from classic Arabic, *hazz* or *qazz*, which themselves came from the Persian *gaz* or *qaz*, which mean "silk." It is a plain woven cloth that is very loose and open. It can be made of cotton, polyester, nylon, or silk. It is very fine and transparent, light, and very soft. It is used for making dress clothing.

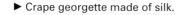

▲ Satin crape made of silk.

▶ Crape georgette made of silk.

Organdy

Organdy is a plain woven cotton cloth with very fine threads and a very dense and regular weave. It is submitted to a special chemical treatment that modifies the characteristics of the fibers, making it stiff and transparent. Organdy fabrics wrinkle easily, unless they have been treated. There is an imitation organdy that is treated with a starch to make it stiff, but it disappears when washed. Organdy is used for making curtains, flowers, decorations, and dresses.

Organza

This name comes from the Italian *organza*, which in turn came from *Urgenc*, a city in Uzbekistan. Organza is similar to organdy; it is made of silk, rayon, or cotton, although organza is nearly always made of cotton. It is different from organdy in that it has a greater number of threads and is therefore denser.

Pongee

This fabric originated in China. It was a brownish or yellowish silk fabric of medium quality made on household looms (*pen-shi*). Also called *habotai*, it is a plain woven silk fabric that is lightweight or medium weight; it has some sheen and is dense and durable, with a soft and smooth texture. It is also made with cotton or rayon.

▶ Silk pongee.

▼ Cotton fabrics: organza (A), organdy (B), and cambric or chambray (C).

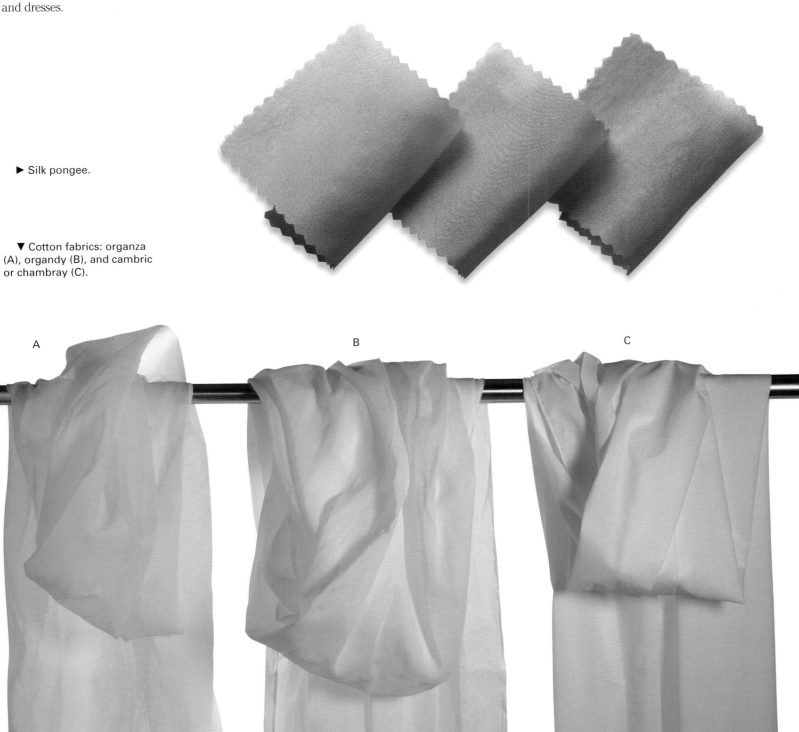

A

B

C

Poplin

The name of this fabric probably comes from the French *popeline*, a version of the Spanish *paplina*, although some authors believe it to be a derivation of "Pope," referring to the head of the Catholic Church because it was first used to manufacture liturgical items and was used when the city of Avignon, France was the papal residence. It is a combed cotton cloth (which purifies and straightens the fibers), with a plain weave, and it is somewhat shiny and very durable. It is also made from a mixture of cotton, silk, wool, and artificial fibers. It is mainly used for making uniforms, shirts, and blouses.

Satin

The word satin is derived from the Latin *seta*, which means silk. It is a flat woven fabric and can be made from silk, cotton, and artificial fibers like rayon or acetate. It has body, is somewhat heavy and soft, and its surface is smooth and lustrous. It is used for high-quality clothing.

Velvet

This fabric is woven with two warp threads and a long, thick weft thread, and the cloth has a closely woven, soft, and fluffy side perpendicular to the surface of the fabric. The weave can be seen on the other side of the cloth. Velvet can be made from silk, acetate, rayon, or artificial fibers mixed with wool or combed wool. Generally, the velvets that have silk are made with rayon or cotton thread for the weft, and silk for the warp.

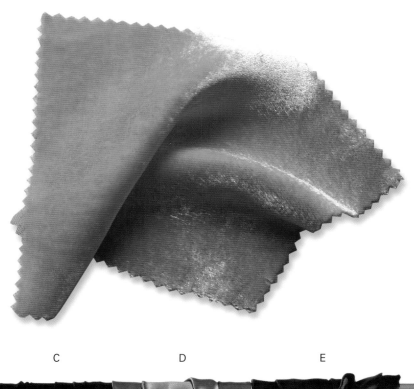

► Velvet with a mixture of rayon and silk.

▼ Artificial fabrics: satin (A, C, D, E) and crape (B).

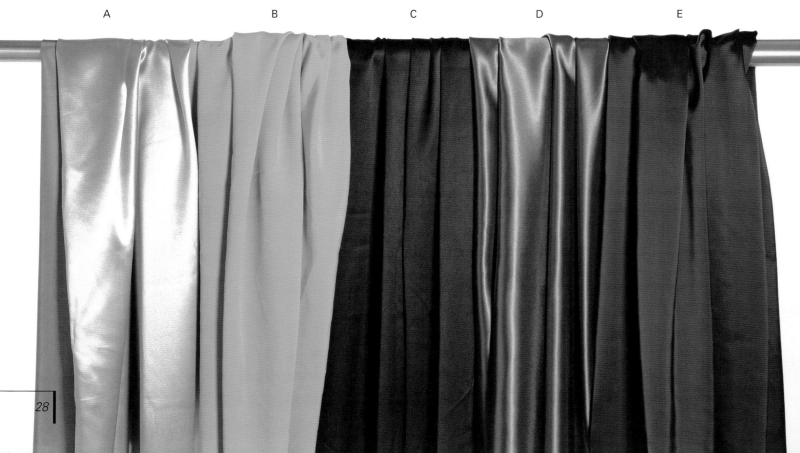

A   B   C   D   E

▼ Silk twill.

▲ Polyester knit.

▲ Cotton knit.

▲ Linen knit.

▲ Silk knit.

Twill

Silk fabric with a twill weave is densely woven and very durable, and it will not tear easily. The surface has characteristic diagonal lines.

Knit

Knit fabrics can be made with linen, cotton, silk, artificial fibers, or a mixture of natural and artificial fibers. In all cases, knit fabrics have a direction, that is, the mesh is more or less flexible depending on which direction it is pulled. Knit pieces are more flexible in their width; they can be stretched further than in their length. This characteristic affects the fabric printing process.

▼ Knit fabric (A) is less flexible across the length (B) than the width (C) of the piece.

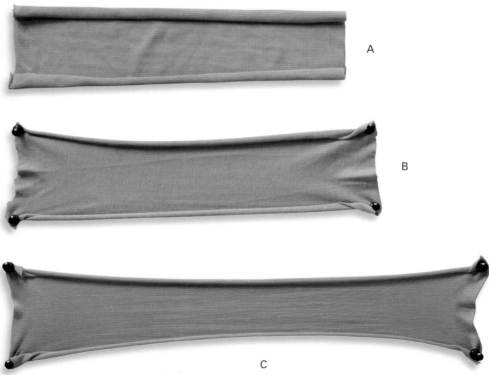

A

B

C

*I*n this chapter we will explain in great detail the tools and materials that are used for printing textiles in the studio. They are grouped according to their use, depending on the technique being used for the job, so that the reader can easily find all the materials and utensils that are required for carrying out each technical process. You will find a description of each one, an explanation of its possible uses, and in cases where it may be required, advice about safety.

Textile printing is a very broad field whose limits are decided by the artist. Formal innovation is becoming a value of this artistic discipline, carrying with it constant research on new approaches and a search for new solutions that make use of known materials and techniques from a new angle. We encourage the readers of this book to look for and develop innovative solutions, gathering as much technical information as possible on the potential of the tools and materials that are used for textile printing.

Materials
and Tools

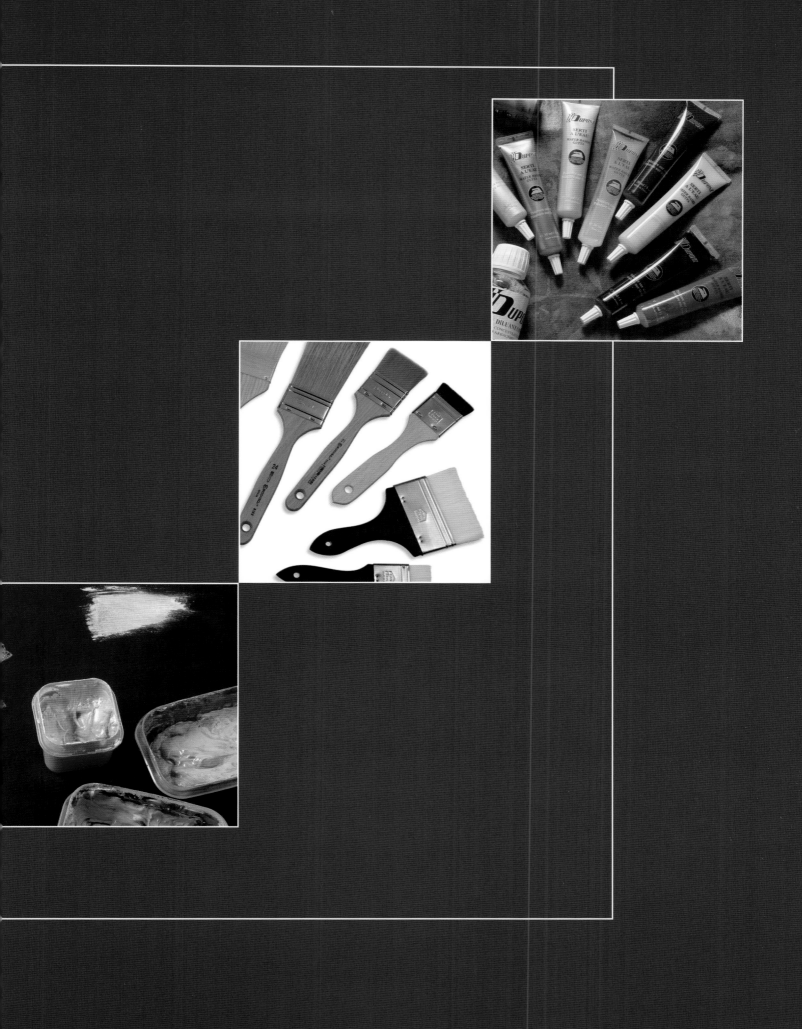

Specific Materials

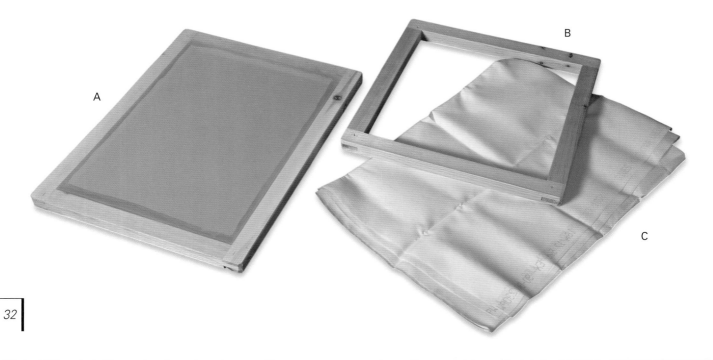

▲ Linoleum.

▲ Voile fabric and screen-printing mesh.

▼ Ready to use commercially made screen (A), commercially made frame (B), and mesh (C).

For Block Printing

Linoleum

This material is made of linseed oil mixed with particles (finely ground dust) of cork, wood, or calcareous rock—among other materials—that are kneaded and applied to a strong, loosely woven jute cloth. The mixture also incorporates pigments and can contain resins from the wood, depending on the manufacturer. It is used to make the printing blocks in place of wood. There are several kinds of linoleum based on their composition and on the manufacturer. Some are harder than others and are therefore more difficult to carve. There is a variety of light linoleum, between bone and gray in color, with a somewhat rough surface, that allows you to create texture on the print.

For Serigraphy

The Frame

The key to successfully creating a silk-screened image is a well-made screen. Screens for serigraphy are made of a stretched mesh attached to a frame that acts as a support. The frames can be made of wood or aluminum; the latter is used in industrial printing. In any case, they must have parallel sides and be rigid, stable when holding the tension of the screen, light enough so that they can be used efficiently, and resistant to the chemical products that are used in this technique.

Wood frames are less expensive and function very well for studio work. They are light and easy to handle and construct, and they allow the screen to be attached without problems. Wood is the raw material used to make frames, which will not harm the environment because the wood is recyclable. It is possible to construct the frames in your studio, or you can buy them from specialty stores. Either way, it is important that they be of good quality, with wide wood pieces and mortise and tenon joints at the corners so the frames will be as strong and stable as possible. An option that is less expensive than commercially made silk screen frames are the stretchers made for paintings, but they are not as strong as actual frames made for serigraphy.

Mesh

Mesh is the fundamental part of the silk screen. There is a great variety of meshes, some specifically made for industrial use, from which you must choose the most appropriate based on the work that is to be done. In choosing a mesh you must first consider the design that you wish to print, the ink that you will be using, and the fabric to be printed; then consider its size, composition, and the diameter of the threads and the openings between the threads of the mesh. For some industrial work and for jobs that require a great amount of detail, a screen called 120-mesh (120 threads per centimeter), is used, although mesh with a lower thread count is also often used. The higher the thread count, the more closely woven the mesh and the better the detail of the printing. The mesh should be durable and resistant to the chemicals that are used in screen printing. Nylon mesh resists alkaline

▲ Reversible adhesive in aerosol form (A), emulsion (B), sensitizer liquid ready for mixing (C), turpentine solvent (D), opaque marker (E).

solutions but is sensitive to acidic solutions and humidity, while polyester mesh is resistant to humidity and acids and is recommended for studio work. The greatest inconvenience of screen-printing mesh is its cost. In your studio a closely woven polyester fabric known as voile can be used as a substitute for commercial serigraphy mesh. It is generally reliable for printing, but as in all cases, the thread count of the voile should be taken into account based on the specific needs of each printing job. Keep in mind that the use of open meshes with low thread counts can be used to create very expressive work, since they allow you to create interesting effects.

Emulsion

Serigraphic emulsion is photosensitive and hardens when it is exposed to direct light. Emulsions are sold in containers, one with the colored emulsion (opaque and well-sealed) and the other with a sensitizer, to mix in the studio at the moment when their use is required. The method of preparation depends on the brand, so it is important to read the instructions before mixing. This should always be done in a controlled environment, free from dust, with low light and a yellow light source that will not sensitize the emulsion. Generally, manufacturers sell the sensitizer in powder form that must be mixed with water, although some sell it in liquid form, ready to be mixed with the emulsion. When you are ready the sensitizer is mixed with the emulsion, and it is allowed to rest

until the bubbles completely disappear; some manufacturers recommend allowing it to rest for sixty minutes. After applying it to the mesh it should be left to dry horizontally in a dust-free, dark, and temperature-controlled environment for the amount of time indicated by the manufacturer. The length of time it is exposed to the light will depend on the type of light, the distance from it, the amount of emulsion on the screen, and the type of mesh.

All emulsions will last a year from the time of manufacture if they are kept in their well-sealed original container. It is usually recommended to store them at temperatures below 68°F (20°C), and some companies suggest you keep their product in the refrigerator. Sensitized emulsions should be used right away, although some manufacturers claim that they can be kept for some time in a tightly sealed container. You should request the technical specification sheet from the maker and follow the instructions closely regarding storage, preparation, and safety, as well as the safe disposal of leftover product.

Opaque Marker

Permanent opaque markers can be used for creating original designs, marking directly on an acetate sheet that will be the template for the motif that will be printed on the screen.

Reversible Adhesive

Reversible adhesive in aerosol cans is temporary, allowing you to momentarily attach the fabric to the work surface efficiently and keep it from moving during the printing process. It does not stain or leave marks on the fabric.

Paint and Solvent

Acrylic enamel paints are used to seal the wood frames. The wood tends to absorb water and chemicals, and it can swell and later shrink, causing the frame of the screen to twist and warp. The acrylic paints are applied directly to the wood and then allowed to dry before attaching the mesh. Using paints of different colors allows you to personalize the screens in studios shared by several artists, or to identify different series of projects, for example. Each kind of paint requires its own specific solvent.

▶ Acrylic paints.

For Batik

Beeswax

Beeswax is also sometimes called natural wax. It is a secretion of the glands of bees; it is a transparent liquid when secreted but becomes semisolid when it comes into contact with air. The color of beeswax varies from yellow to coffee-colored tones to black. It is used in the studio to prepare the wax that is used to make the reserves required for the batik printing technique. It is sold in blocks and in pellets. It is usually melted and mixed with an equal amount of paraffin, that is, in a 1:1 ratio of beeswax to paraffin. However, you can also mix 70 percent paraffin with 30 percent beeswax. The latter, after it cools, is elastic, flexible, and dense; when mixed with the paraffin it can be used to create the designs and patterns on the fabric.

Solid Paraffin

This is a derivative of petroleum, a mixture of hydrocarbons, that is white and translucent. It is mixed with beeswax to create the wax used for doing batik in the studio. The paraffin adds hardness to the mixture after it has cooled and is brittle, which creates very fine cracking effects.

Commercial Wax

Batik wax can also be purchased for immediate use. Manufacturers sell this wax for designing in blocks, powder, and pellets, ready to be melted. Depending on the company, the wax will have different melting temperatures and different properties. For example, it can be more or less brittle for different cracking effects. There are special waxes for making different kinds of cracking. These are somewhat more porous and brittle waxes than those used for the design, and they create a prominent cracking pattern over large surfaces.

Salt

Salt is sodium chloride (NaCl), a compound used as a condiment. In the studio it is used in solution, to fix the dyes in cotton fabrics. When working with silk it is used in crystal form to create very interesting effects, sprinkling it on the surface of the fabric while the dyes or paints are still wet. The salt absorbs the paint or dye, creating gradations of color and sinuous shapes.

Vinegar

Vinegar is a sour liquid made from acidic fermented wine, whose main component is acetic acid. It is diluted with water to fix dye and paint on silk, and also to fix ink on wool. It is also used in the bleaching process as an auxiliary material, mixed with water that is used to neutralize the bleach.

Detergent for Silk

This is a special detergent for silk that is used to wash the work after the dye or paint has been fixed. It is used to eliminate excess color and prevent staining, that is, to keep dark colors from staining the lighter ones, and to keep them from running. You will generally use 3$^1/_2$ tablespoons (50 ml) of detergent in 1 gallon (4 L) of warm water, although the proportions depend on the manufacturer. Vinegar may be used in its place.

Disappearing Ink Pen

This is used for drawing designs on all types of fabrics and for marking the placement of the blocks when printing repeated patterns. It has a special nontoxic ink that disappears on contact with water, paints, and ink, or after a period of time that ranges from two to fourteen days, depending on the fiber of the textile and the amount of humidity in the environment. The color should never be fixed by steaming or ironing, or by dry cleaning the fabric before removing the marks or allowing them to disappear, or else they will be permanently fixed in the fabric.

For Devoré

Devoré is based on the use of a paste with the consistency of a gel that has the ability to dissolve vegetable fibers, which in large part consist of cellulose, and leaving the other fibers of the textile intact. There are different formulas for making the devoré gel in the studio, although it is possible to buy it ready-made (by DuPont), which simplifies the process. Commercial devoré paste comes in two containers, one with the paste and the other with the activator in powdered form. They are mixed in a proportion of 85 percent gel to 15 percent activator in a glass or plastic container, stirring with a wood or plastic utensil. After mixing it can be used immediately or kept for later use in a sealed container for up to eight days. It can be applied to textiles using block printing or screen-printing, or with a brush. It is mainly used to create three-dimensional effects on mixed textiles like velvet, but it is possible to create other effects such as opening in cotton fabrics. This product should be mixed and used in a well-ventilated space because it can irritate the respiratory system, and gloves should be used if there is a chance that it will come into contact with your hands. In the studio it should be kept in a locked cabinet.

▼ Paraffin (A), beeswax (B), commercial wax for batik (C), wax prepared in the studio (D), devoré activator (E), vinegar (G), detergent for silk (H), salt (I), disappearing ink pen (J).

For Serti

Gutta

Gutta comes from the Malay words *getah*, which means rubber, and *percha*, which means tree. It is latex derived from the excretions of various species of trees of the *palaquium* genus, particularly from the *P. gutta*, which originated in Southeast Asia and is now grown in Asia and Oceania. The latex is somewhat brown, translucent, and flexible and is similar to rubber, which—like gutta—is an isoprene polymer. Refined and prepared gutta is used in the serti technique for making reserves and outlining shapes to control the distribution of the paint and to separate the painted areas. It is sold in ready-to-use form. There are two kinds of gutta preparations, one made with gasoline and the other with water. The gutta made with gasoline becomes an integral part of the work because it does not disappear when the piece is steamed or washed, but it can be removed by dry cleaning. Gutta made with water is less permanent, so it will not withstand too many layers of paint. When the silk is fixed it disappears with the washing and is not part of the final work.

Gutta is sold in various colors: natural (it looks milky), which creates a colorless reserve; pearly, which has a satin look when dry; and metallic, which dries with a shiny, metallic surface. They are sold in small containers with applicators for direct use, and in larger containers from which the smaller applicators can be filled.

Gutta Solvent

This is a mineral solvent for the guttas made with gasoline (both the transparent and the colored versions). It is used to thin the gutta for working, and it can also be used to remove the no-flow primer (anti-diffusant liquid).

Thickener

Made from a solution of vegetable gum, this is used for fixing and thickening the paint. It is water-soluble and transparent, and it is mixed in a proportion of 25 percent up to 50 percent of the paint, depending on the effect that you wish to achieve. It is used for freehand painting on silk, although it is not good for very detailed work. The lines it makes on silk can be used for certain painterly effects like glazing. It can also be used for printing using the serigraphy process. It is quite slow drying and causes the silk to wrinkle, which can be eliminated by washing.

Solvent

Solvent is used for thinning and lightening colors for silk, softening the tone of the paint. It is sold as a concentrate or in ready-to-use form. The latter is usually mixed with paint in up to a 50 percent proportion, although this depends on the type of paint and the tone you wish to create. The concentrate is prepared by mixing about 1 teaspoon (40 ml) of concentrated solvent with one quart (1 L) of water, preferably distilled, and then adding

the paint until reaching the desired tone. The solvent retards drying and makes it easier for the paint to flow on the silk, which allows you to create different shades and tones of a color as well as multiple effects like gradations and transparencies, and to clean areas with no bleeding paint. It is also used for correcting or removing mistakes made during the painting session.

No-Flow Primer (Anti-Diffusant)

This product is used for preparing the silk for direct freehand painting. It is applied to the silk and forms a thin colorless film that keeps the paint from bleeding on the fabric. It dries quickly and makes the fabric slightly stiff and affects the way it hangs. No-flow primer is available with a gasoline or a water base. The first must be removed by a specialized dry cleaner, while the second can be removed by washing.

Sugar

Sugar can be substituted for salt to achieve similar effects on the surface of the fabric. Like salt, it absorbs the paint or dye and causes gradations in the tones and sinuous shapes.

For Bleaching

Methylcellulose Glue

This product is based on methylcellulose, the main polysaccharide in the fibrous structure of vegetable materials. Cellulose is a very chemically stable molecule that is insoluble in water and hygroscopic, that is, it absorbs water and swells. Methylcellulose glue is an inert, nontoxic adhesive that is safe for people and the environment and is primarily used for gluing paper. The glue is prepared by dissolving it in water, and when it dries it does not show through the paper. In bleaching tasks it is used as a vehicle in the elaboration of the bleaching paste, mixed with water and bleach.

Starch

Starch is a polysaccharide obtained from the seeds of cereals. Cornstarch can be used as a vehicle for making the paste used for bleaching, in place of methylcellulose.

Bleach

This is the common name of sodium hypochlorite (NaClO). It is a transparent liquid that is slightly yellow, with a characteristic pungent odor. It is a powerful disinfectant and oxidizer, as well as an effective bleaching agent since it destroys many of the dyes used for textiles. It is the agent we will use for bleaching tasks. After achieving the desired effect, its action is neutralized by rinsing the textile in abundant running water, and, if required, it can then be soaked in a solution of about 7 fluid ounces (200 ml) of vinegar per quart (1 L) of water.

▼ Cornstarch (A), sugar (B), methylcellulose glue (C), bleach (D), gutta solvent (E), thickener (F), no-flow primer (G), transparent gutta (H), concentrated solvent (I), metallic, transparent, and colored water-base gutta (J).

Pastes and Dyes

Print Base Paste

This paste, also called print base, is the base to which pigments are added so they can be printed on textiles. It is an acrylic paste that can be used like other pigmented pastes for printing with blocks or screens. It is formulated of water-soluble acrylic resins and other components, such as binders, oil-based or synthetic thickeners, and other additives that modify specific properties. It has a creamy consistency, is semi-fluid, and has a milky appearance. If it is applied to a light fabric it is transparent, but on a dark fabric it makes a faint print that is whitish and somewhat transparent, allowing the color of the fabric to show through, which makes for interesting effects. It is also used as a vehicle or base when it is necessary to mix colors with different pastes.

Printing Inks

Printing inks are pastes to which pigments mixed with water (and, in some cases, other products that confer special properties) have been added. Most of the inks used in the studio are water-based and have added synthetic thickeners without solvents. Since they are water based they can be cleaned as long as they have not begun to dry. There are also pastes with a turpentine or water base that contain other solvents besides water. They are flammable, emit noxious odors, contaminate the air and water, and are expensive, which is why they are mainly for industrial use. The water-based pastes are fixed by the polymerization of the acrylic components through a chemical reaction during drying; therefore, they are known as self-fixing paints. Generally, printed textiles can be stacked after three hours, although curing is not completed until seventy-two to ninety-six hours after the printing process, depending on the environmental conditions of the studio. These times vary according to the manufacturer and brand. Although polymer pastes air dry, it is recommended to iron the reverse side of the fabric after it is dry to help fix it, and to not fold it or wash it for at least fifteen days. The pastes should be stored in a tightly sealed container after use, in a cool area of the studio far from any heat sources. During use the container should not be open for too long, since the surface of the product will begin to dry.

Printing pastes can be dye, lacquer, or even have special characteristics like relief paste.

Dyes

Dyes are pigmented pastes that are not very dense, so they are used on light-colored fabrics; the results are prints with transparent tones. They have a creamy consistency and are not as dense as lacquers. Like lacquers, it is possible to make mixtures of different colors to create a desired tone. For making any mixture, use print base and begin adding small amounts of the different colors. Like all printing pastes, this will dry quickly, and if it dries on the printing screen or printing block it will be very difficult to remove. It is a good idea not to take breaks during the printing

▼ Print base and a screen-printed design printed on a dark fabric.

◀ Printing dyes and a screen-printed design on a white textile.

Paint

Paint is a fluid paste composed of one or more pigments mixed with an agglutinate. Textile paints are mainly a mixture of pigments in an emulsion with acrylic (synthetic) agglutinates with a water base, although the components vary depending on the manufacturer and the product. Most of the paints can be diluted with water, since they are water-soluble until they begin to dry. The paints polymerize as they dry. After the printing process has been completed, the fabric should be allowed to dry for at least twenty-four hours, and after this time has passed it can be ironed on the reverse side for three minutes, although the instructions may vary from one manufacturer to another. They are not toxic, they can be mixed to create any desired color, and they are used for block printing and for painting the textiles directly with a brush. The paint is deposited on the textile fibers and makes them somewhat stiff, although recently, paints have been developed that leave the fabrics more flexible to the touch. Depending on the brand and the type of paint, they can be applied to different kinds of textile fibers like silk, cotton, and synthetic. A wide range of fabric paints are available: transparent ones that do not cover the weave; very dense opaque ones; pearlescent paints with iridescent reflections; and fluorescent or metallic paints.

process, and once you have finished you should wash the screen or block with a great amount of running water until the product is completely removed.

Lacquer

Lacquers are pigmented pastes that are very dense and can be used for printing on dark-colored textiles. They are opaque colors that cover the original tone of the base fabric; the print has a certain amount of relief to the touch. It is possible to make mixtures to create any desired tone. They have a thick consistency, are denser than dyes, and are more difficult to use than dyes when used for screen printing. They also dry faster, so they cannot be used for screen printing for long periods of time.

Relief Paste

Relief paste (also called puff, or expanded paint) is a pigmented paste that has the property of inflating to several times its original volume when heated to create a relief effect. It is a somewhat dense paste that can be applied to light or dark fabrics because of their dense and opaque color. After they have been printed they should be allowed to dry for twenty minutes (depending on the conditions in the studio), although it is recommended to let them dry for several hours since applying heat while

they are still damp can cause problems of solidity and durability when washed. After they have dried, heat is applied by ironing the fabric from one to three minutes at 265 to 285°F (130 to 140°C) on the back, while protecting the front with a clean white cloth. In the presence of heat the paste will swell from eight to twelve times in volume to create a pronounced relief. The best results are achieved with cotton fabrics, but relief paste can be used on textiles manufactured from any fiber.

▼ Fabric paint and a block-printed design on a light-colored fabric.

Paints for Silk

These paints are specially made for painting on silk fibers. They are also called dyes and are very fluid paints that quickly spread on the fabric. Thin and translucent, when applied they are rapidly absorbed by the fibers that are soon soaked with the color. They do not make the fabric stiff, and after they are fixed the colors are bright. Most of the paints are mixed with an alcohol base and are nontoxic. There are two main groups of paints: those fixed by steaming and those fixed by ironing. The first are usually made with an alcohol base and have a large concentration of pigments, which results in very bright colors. They are available in a wide range of colors, even in pastel and opaque tones. The colors of the second group are not as bright, but they are easier to work with. There are other varieties that use a fixative that is applied to the dried paint and left to work for one hour, after which they are rinsed with water. There are also some brands of paint that are fixed by drying. After they have been applied they can be considered fixed after twelve to twenty-four hours.

◀ Paints for silk and a brushstroke on silk fabric.

Dyes

Dyes are colored substances that permanently color textiles. The fabrics can be submerged in a bath to color them, although in some cases they can also be painted with the colors. The dyes penetrate the fibers of the textile to form, after fixing, a chemical bond. Unlike paint, they do not stiffen the fabric. Dyes can be natural, the majority of which require a mordant to fix them in the textiles, or they can be synthetic. The natural dyes can be of animal origin, like the marine snails of the genus *murex*, which produce the color purple, or the cochineal, which gives us the color crimson. Or they can be vegetable, like the plants that give us indigo, the onionskin that produces a yellowish color, or the skin of the walnut that makes brown and black tones; or even minerals like iron oxide that give us the color red. Synthetic dyes are artificial products based on different elements mixed in a laboratory. Aniline dyes were the first to be developed and are sold as powders or liquids. In all cases it is important to follow the manufacturer's recommendations when it comes to amounts, preparation of the textile, fixatives, and instructions for use. You should also pay attention to the information on safety and safe removal of residues.

◀▲ Direct dyes (A) and reactive dyes (B).

Synthetic Dyes

There are different kinds of synthetic dyes; the most common are acid dyes and reactive dyes. Acid dyes are used for coloring fibers of animal origin such as silk and wool, as well as other protein and polyamide fabrics. Their use requires a heated acid medium to fix them to the fibers. They have bright colors and are generally easy to use. Reactive dyes, more commonly utilized, are used for dyeing animal fibers such as silk and wool, and vegetable fibers (cellulosic) such as cotton, linen, sisal, and others like viscose and rayon. As the name suggests, these dyes react chemically with the fibers of the textile and form covalent links with them. In the covalent links the atoms of medium and great electronegativity (atoms that have a tendency to acquire electrons) can share electrons when they are joined with each other. Each one will donate one electron of the pair that characterizes this kind of link. Thanks to the type of link that is established between the atoms of the dye and those of the fibers, the textiles colored with this dye posses excellent resistance to light and washing. They are generally used cold, along with salt and a fixative (an alkali, usually sodium carbonate). In the case of dyeing wool, hot water is used and vinegar is substituted for the salt.

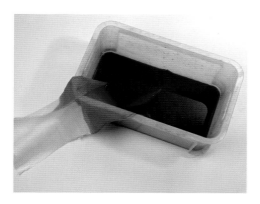

▲ The fabrics are submerged in a previously prepared dye.

Direct dyes are used to color the fibers without the need of much preparation or the use of mordant. They are used for dyeing cotton, linen, silk, wool, viscose, and nylon fibers, among others. They are easy to find and inexpensive, but they must be used with salt and boiling water during the entire coloring process. As in the previous case, vinegar should be substituted for salt if you are dyeing wool.

Regardless of the dye being used, it will render different results depending on the fiber used in making the textile, so you must consider this factor before beginning.

Selective Dyes

Selective dyes are a special case among synthetic dyes. These are combinations of two dyes that are used at the same time, in the same session for fabrics made of two different fibers. These are sold in liquid form in various types of containers, and they are mainly used for dyeing velvet pieces that have previously been worked with devoré, to highlight and emphasize the relief. One of the components dyes the viscose and cotton fibers—that is, the cellulosic fibers—while the other dyes the fibers with protein components, like silk and wool. The dyes are mixed with water and a special fixative developed by the manufacturer, as well as with salt and vinegar.

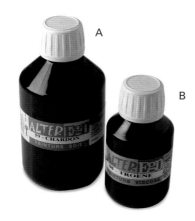

▲ The two components of selective dyes: dye for silk and wool (A), and dye for viscose and cotton (B).

◄ The same dye offers different results depending on the fiber of the textile: cotton (A), wool (B), silk (C), and velvet made of viscose and silk (D).

Auxiliary Materials

Acetate and Paper

Acetate Sheet

Acetate film was first manufactured from cellulose acetate, which was colorless and transparent. It is mainly used in design for overlaying a motif on a base design or for making transparencies for projectors. In printing it is used for the originals that are later burned onto photosensitive silk screens with a bright light.

Tracing Paper

This paper is modified with sulfuric acid to become translucent. It is very smooth, is dense with an even texture, has a certain amount of surface hardness, and is somewhat resistant to humidity, although excessive water will cause it to buckle. It is used for designing, for sketching, and for transferring designs. It is mainly used in serigraphy for making an original (directly or photocopied onto another paper) that will be burned onto a printing screen with a bright light.

Carbon Paper

This paper has carbon on one side and is used in the block printing process for copying the pattern or original design onto a linoleum block.

Blotter Paper

Blotter paper is quite thick, heavy, and spongy, and it has no glue sizing. It is used for absorbing water or the possible traces of liquids during the work session, such as inks and paste.

Kraft Paper

This is also known as wrapping paper. It can be white or brown, is very durable, and is widely used for wrapping and shipping. It is used in the studio for protecting the work surface from spills, and the brown paper is also used for wrapping fabrics that are being steam fixed.

▲ Tracing paper.

Adhesive Tape and Glue

Adhesive Tape

Common adhesive tape is used for joining and fixing papers. During the creative process they are used for joining parts of the design and attaching them to a paper support. It is also used for correcting some defects in the emulsion on silk screens after they have been exposed to light, covering small areas where the emulsion did not adhere or was damaged.

Shipping Tape

This is adhesive tape made from plastic that is used for fixing kraft paper and blotter paper on the work surface.

▼ Blotter paper (A), normal paper (B), tracing paper (C), kraft paper (D), shipping tape (E), and gummed paper tape (F).

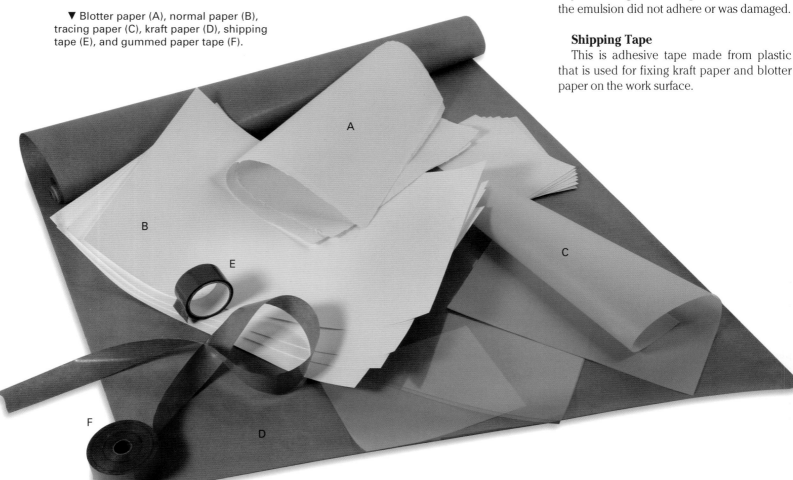

Gummed Paper Tape

This is a variety of kraft paper that has one side covered with an adhesive that becomes sticky when it is moistened. Generally used for framing, this covers the area where the mesh joins the frame of the printing screen to keep the ink or paint from leaking onto the fabric. The gummed paper tape can also be used to cover any space or joint not covered by the emulsion.

Contact Cement

Contact cement is used to glue the mesh of the serigraphy screen and keep it from moving. As indicated by its name, it adheres on contact. It is made with a synthetic gum base (usually neoprene) dissolved in a solvent, which will evaporate and leave the hardened adhesive. It should be used in a well-ventilated space and kept away from heat sources. It is thick and has strong adhesive power, and after drying it is very durable. It requires seventy-two hours to completely dry.

White Glue

This is also known as carpenter's glue. Polyvinyl acetate (CH_3COO $CH:CH_2$), commonly called PVA, is made of transparent resins, soluble in some organic solvents, that have a strong adhesive power. They form very flexible films, are resistant to light, and are unaffected by many chemicals. In printing they are mainly used for covering small defects in the emulsion on printing screens that have been exposed to light. They can also be used to directly create reserves on silk screens. They dry completely in twenty-four hours.

For Designing

It is a good idea to have a large selection of drawing and painting materials in the studio for designing projects and even creating originals for printing. Pencils, markers, and charcoal are used for making designs, which can be colored with pencils, watercolor pencils, pastels, and paints like gouache, acrylics, and watercolors. Gouache and acrylics can also be used to create original designs for serigraphy. Opaque ink can also be used for creating originals for screen printing.

Other Materials

Nylon Sock

Pieces of clean nylon stockings and nylon socks can be used to line a strainer to clean the wax used for make reserves in the batik technique, separating out any particles. Some of these particles could pass through a typical strainer, so the sock is used because it is fine enough to eliminate any leftover solid.

Denatured Alcohol

This alcohol (CH_3OH) is also called methanol, methyl alcohol, or wood alcohol. It is a colorless liquid, although it is sold with color added, has an odor, is very volatile and flammable, and highly toxic if ingested or inhaled. It is used in an alcohol lamp for heating wax inside the batik needle used for making reserves.

▲ Adhesive tape (A), contact cement (B), and nylon sock (C).

◀ Opaque ink.

◀ Materials for creating originals: pencils, markers, erasers, graphite, chalk, kneaded erasers, blending sticks, etc.

Special Tools

For Block Printing with Linoleum

Chisels

Chisels are tools that are used for carving linoleum blocks. They have a tempered steel tip (usually chromium molybdenum) that is available in many shapes, and a wood handle. One end of the steel tip is shaped to fit inside a collar that is part of the handle. The tip itself is sharpened at the other end, and it is used for cutting the linoleum.

Chisels for cutting linoleum have short handles and tips, unlike chisels designed for cutting wood. Some have an ergonomic handle in the shape of a mushroom, designed to fit comfortably in the palm of the hand.

There are chisels with interchangeable tips. They have a plastic handle with a collar that holds the tips, which can be removed by pressing on a rod at the end of the handle. This allows you to change the tips as needed.

There are many kinds of chisels with cutting edges that make different shapes in the linoleum, and the models of chisel vary from one manufacturer to another, so it is possible to find a very wide assortment on the market. It is easy to find an appropriate chisel for any kind of work.

Printing Press

The press is used for printing the design on the linoleum block onto the textile. It consists of a rectangular platen mounted between two cylinders, which apply pressure that can be adjusted with two screws located at each end of the upper cylinder. It is attached to a chassis of heavy rigid steel with ball bearings that allow the platen to move easily between the two cylinders. The screws are used to level the cylinders following a scale that is engraved in the frame of the press. It is very important that they be perfectly leveled and parallel to make acceptable prints. There are many kinds of presses; the least expensive are tabletop models. They generally do not have reductive gears and their cylinders measure from 2 to 4 inches or even 6 inches (5 cm to 10 or 15 cm). The lower cylinder is lined or textured on the surface to help it grab. They can accommodate a platen up to 16 inches wide by 32 inches long (41 cm by 80 cm). The maximum opening between the cylinders is 2 inches (5 cm), and they are controlled by a wheel or spokes. They can be fixed to the tabletop with a removable clamp that can be screwed down to anchor it firmly. The platen is made of fiber and is stiff and free of deformities.

◄ Chisels with wood handles and different tips (A), a chisel with interchangeable tips and a plastic handle (B), different interchangeable tips (C).

▼ Tabletop press without reduction gears, controlled with four spokes.

There are presses with incorporated legs and tables that have reduction gears and cylinders of greater diameter that will accommodate larger platens and are operated with eight spokes or a wheel.

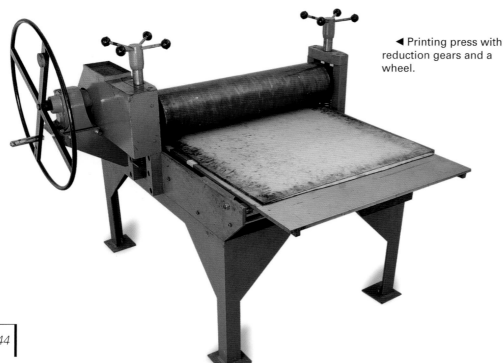

◄ Printing press with reduction gears and a wheel.

For Serigraphy

Exposure Unit

This machine hardens the photosensitive emulsion on serigraphy screens through direct exposure to bright ultraviolet light. In essence, an exposure unit is formed of a metal frame with an ultraviolet light source (fluorescent tubes that emit light from the ultraviolet spectrum, halogen lights, or similar light sources) on the bottom, separated at a specific distance by a clear glass sheet, with a rubber-lined top and a vacuum suction motor. It is a good idea to have one or two yellow incandescent bulbs located near the UV light source to help you correctly locate the screen. There are usually different controls for each function: one for turning the vacuum pump off and on, one for turning the UV lights on, and one for the yellow lights.

There are tabletop exposure units for small screens that are inexpensive and very easy to use. They are usually for screens from 24 by 24 inches to 30 by 36 inches (60 by 60 cm to 75 by 90 cm), and they have a complete control panel for all the functions.

Compact exposure units are larger, and they are good for studios that have a large workload. They can have fluorescent tubes or halogen lamps and digital control panels that control the brightness and exposure time, a digital chronometer, an electronic vacuum meter, and a control for the pump.

Arm Screen

This is a metal tool consisting of a moveable arm. It has a counterweight at one end and a support with clamps at the other, joined in the middle where there is a screw that allows you to set the height and a clamp that attaches the tool to the work surface. It is used for print runs, that is, screening the same design on a number of pieces of clothing, such as T-shirts.

For Silk

Steamer

This tool is used for fixing paints that require steam. It consists of a long, hollow, stainless steel cylinder with a thermometer on top that is graduated from 30° to 250°F (0° to 120°C), and at the bottom has a small valve through which the steam escapes. There is a support at the bottom to guarantee stability. The textile is placed inside the steamer after first rolling it around a stainless steel bar that is made to fit the steamer. The process requires an electric heater, a pressure cooker, a rubber tube, and a flat pot. The cylinder is placed on the flat pot with a little water, then the pressure cooker is filled with water and the escape valve for the steam is attached to the valve of the steamer with the rubber hose. When the cooker is heated the water vapor is directed to the inside of the steamer.

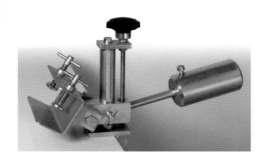

◀ Arm screen.

▼ Compact exposure unit.

◀ Steamer setup: hotplate, pressure cooker, rubber hose, flat pot, steamer with its support, and the bar for wrapping the fabric.

Holding, Fixing, and Stretching

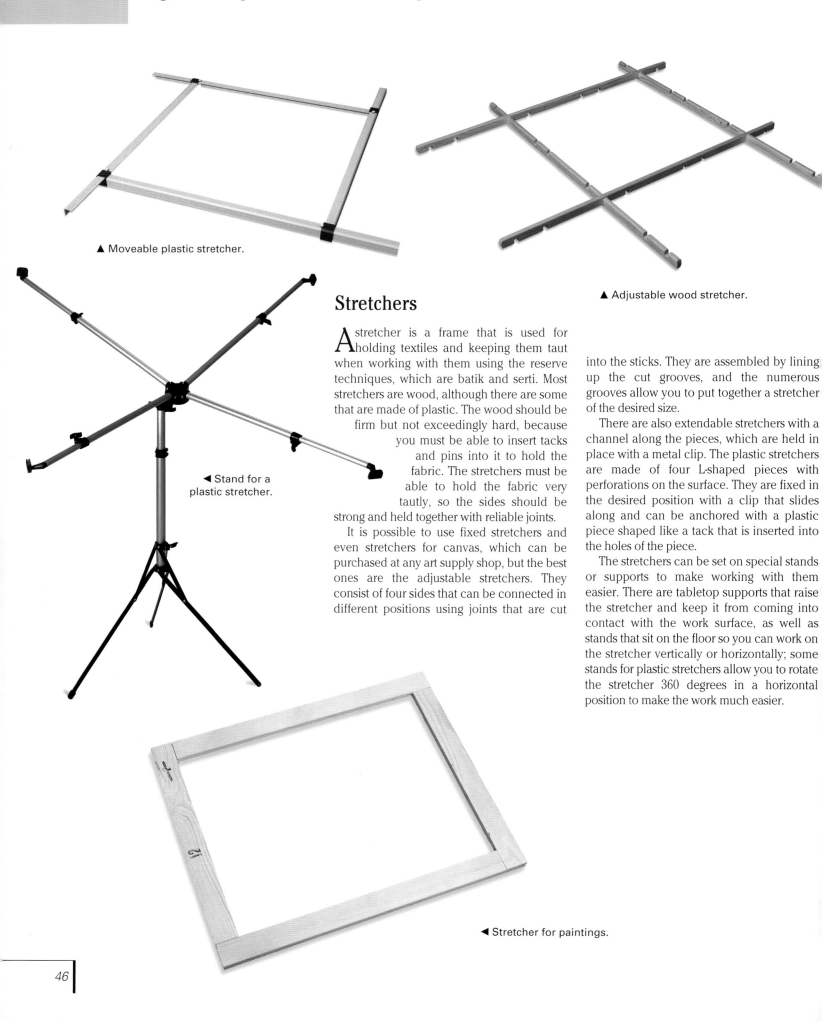

▲ Moveable plastic stretcher.

▲ Adjustable wood stretcher.

Stretchers

◄ Stand for a plastic stretcher.

A stretcher is a frame that is used for holding textiles and keeping them taut when working with them using the reserve techniques, which are batik and serti. Most stretchers are wood, although there are some that are made of plastic. The wood should be firm but not exceedingly hard, because you must be able to insert tacks and pins into it to hold the fabric. The stretchers must be able to hold the fabric very tautly, so the sides should be strong and held together with reliable joints.

It is possible to use fixed stretchers and even stretchers for canvas, which can be purchased at any art supply shop, but the best ones are the adjustable stretchers. They consist of four sides that can be connected in different positions using joints that are cut into the sticks. They are assembled by lining up the cut grooves, and the numerous grooves allow you to put together a stretcher of the desired size.

There are also extendable stretchers with a channel along the pieces, which are held in place with a metal clip. The plastic stretchers are made of four L-shaped pieces with perforations on the surface. They are fixed in the desired position with a clip that slides along and can be anchored with a plastic piece shaped like a tack that is inserted into the holes of the piece.

The stretchers can be set on special stands or supports to make working with them easier. There are tabletop supports that raise the stretcher and keep it from coming into contact with the work surface, as well as stands that sit on the floor so you can work on the stretcher vertically or horizontally; some stands for plastic stretchers allow you to rotate the stretcher 360 degrees in a horizontal position to make the work much easier.

◄ Stretcher for paintings.

Other Tools

Stapler

The mechanism in a manual stapler allows you to firmly insert staples into a surface. The staples are made of wire in a U-shape that will hold an object or part of an object firmly in place. The stapler is used to attach the mesh to the frame when making screens for serigraphy.

Clothespins

Wood clothespins are used to hold the textiles when hanging them to dry.

Canvas Stretching Pliers

These steel pliers have rectangular jaws with indentations that fit into each other when closed. They are used by painters to hold and stretch the canvas on the stretcher. In textile printing they are used to stretch the mesh when making printing screens.

Fabric Suspension Claw Hooks

These hooks are used to stretch and hold the fabric to the stretcher. They are made of three metal hooks on the front, with a plastic frame on the back. They are held to the stretcher with rubber bands that are pinned to the wood. The hooks have an opening in the plastic part that attaches to the rubber band, and the metal hooks on the other side attach to the fabric. They are used for silk that will be painted up to the edge without leaving any borders (a technique used for scarves).

Thumbtacks

Stainless steel thumbtacks with three points are used to directly attach the fabric to the wood stretcher. Begin by attaching the fabric at one corner, stretching it carefully, and attaching the other three corners.

Pushpins

These are tacks that have a central point and a plastic head. They are used like the previous tacks, but their advantage is that they are much easier to manipulate and attach because of the large head.

U-Shaped Fabric Pins

U-shaped pins are very useful for attaching fabric to the table of a printing surface. Although they can be difficult to find, they are very practical. These pins can be found in very specialized fabrics or notions shops.

▼ Canvas stretching pliers (A), wood clothespins (B), fabric hooks for plastic stretchers (C), pushpins (D), thumbtacks (E), fabric suspension claw hooks (F), U-shaped fabric pins (G), stapler and staples (H).

Applying, Mixing, and Extending

Different Types

Brushes

Brushes are instruments consisting of a bundle of hair held in a metal ferrule that is attached to a handle. There are different brands, materials, and shapes on the market from which to choose the correct brush for each job. They are numbered to indicate the thickness of the tip.

When it comes to the materials, there are hog bristle brushes, sable hair, kolinsky, red sable, mongoose, squirrel, weasel, ox, goat, pony, wolf, and synthetic hair.

Hog bristle brushes are made with bleached boar hair, which is split at the ends and helps hold the paint. Sable hair brushes, like those of mongoose, are very soft, elastic, and durable. Squirrel tail hair is excellent when it comes to softness and absorption.

Weasel hair is also very absorbent, elastic, and resistant to wear, and it always maintains its original form. Ox hair is stiffer and harder than the previous ones and is also less elastic. Wolf hair is very soft and good for working on large surfaces. Brushes made with synthetic hair are very inexpensive and soft, but they are not usually very durable.

When it comes to the shape of the brushes, this will depend on the ferrule, which can be round or flat, and on the length and form of the hair.

Large, wide brushes are rectangular, and most have short and stiff bristles, although there are also some with soft and long hair.

Squeegees

Squeegees are tools made of a long piece of rubber or metal that is inserted in a wood, plastic, or metal handle of a similar length.

They are used in the screen-printing process, for printing and spreading the photosensitive emulsion.

A squeegee with a metal blade is used for spreading photo emulsion on a screen. Printing is done with a squeegee with a rubber blade, which can be neoprene, rubber, or polyurethane. Polyurethane blades are very durable and are made in several colors. The polyurethane blades that are black are very inexpensive but are not very durable and wear out quickly; they can even darken the lighter colors during the printing process. Rubber blades are somewhat more durable, and they are also black. In any case, the squeegee should be as wide as the screen that is being used for printing.

Squeegees made for cleaning windows can be substituted for emulsion and printing squeegees, but are not very durable.

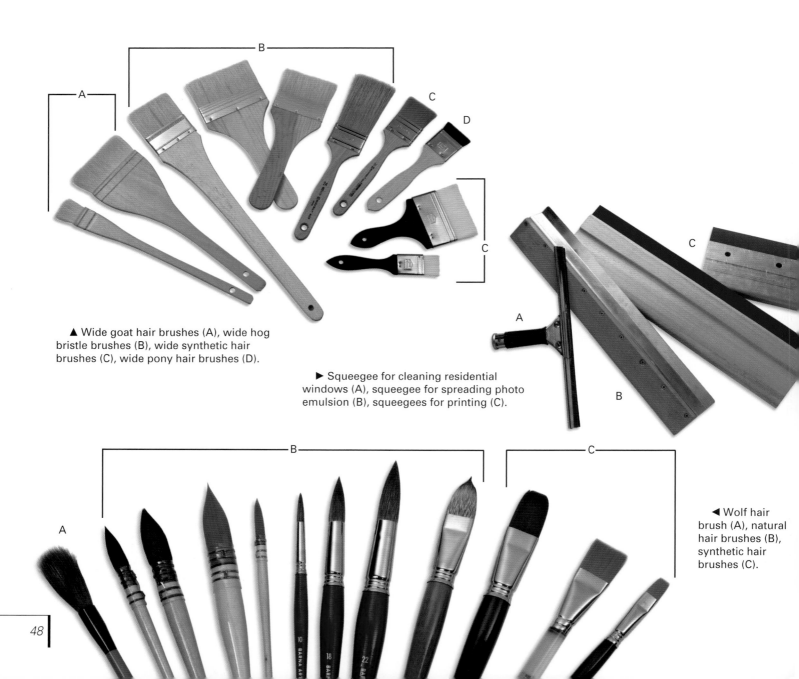

▲ Wide goat hair brushes (A), wide hog bristle brushes (B), wide synthetic hair brushes (C), wide pony hair brushes (D).

► Squeegee for cleaning residential windows (A), squeegee for spreading photo emulsion (B), squeegees for printing (C).

◄ Wolf hair brush (A), natural hair brushes (B), synthetic hair brushes (C).

◀ Tjanting and electric melting pot for wax.

▶ Sponge roller.

▶ Electric tjanting.

◀ Different tjantings.

Tjantings

Tjantings, also known as canting tools, are used for creating reserves in the batik process. These instruments are composed of a wood handle with a small container on one end with one or more spigots or hollow needles. These were originally made of copper, but nowadays they are also made of alloys of different metals. Wax can be introduced into the tjanting in solid form and then heated over an alcohol lamp, or wax that has previously been heated in a melting pot can be used. There are several kinds of electric tjantings, and the most useful ones have a temperature control feature.

Rollers

Rollers are cylinders that are attached to a handle that allows you to hold it and use it comfortably. Rubber rollers are used for pressing the fabric against linoleum blocks that are used for stamping design motifs on fabric. Sponge rollers are used for applying paint or paste to the linoleum blocks used in the printing process.

Sponges

Sponges are used in the serti technique for large applications and making gradations. These should be fine, synthetic sponges attached to a handle. They are available in different shapes and sizes, so you can always choose the most appropriate one for your needs. They are used for applying products like no-flow primer on silk when you wish to paint freehand, for painting the background color of a composition, or for making gradations.

Gutta Applicator

Although most manufacturers sell gutta in containers with applicators that are ready for use, you should always have applicators in the studio. It is more affordable to buy gutta in large containers and then put the necessary amount for each project in an applicator. These are small plastic bottles that are semitransparent and somewhat flexible, with a screw top fitted with a metal spout or nozzle. The spouts come with openings of various sizes, and they can be bought separately and are interchangeable with other applicators. However, it is most practical to have a good selection of applicators, each with its own nozzle. The applicators are supplied with a needle that is used to close the spout and keep the gutta from drying.

Atomizer

This is a small container, often plastic, with an atomizing mechanism that sprays fine drops of liquid when it is depressed. The atomizer can be used for creating interesting effects, since it will spray both ink and paint in a very uniform pattern.

▲ Rubber roller (A), sponge (B), dispenser (C), atomizer (D), gutta applicator (E).

▼ Nozzle for gutta applicator with a needle.

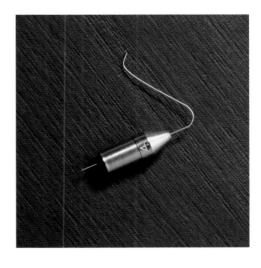

Auxiliary Tools

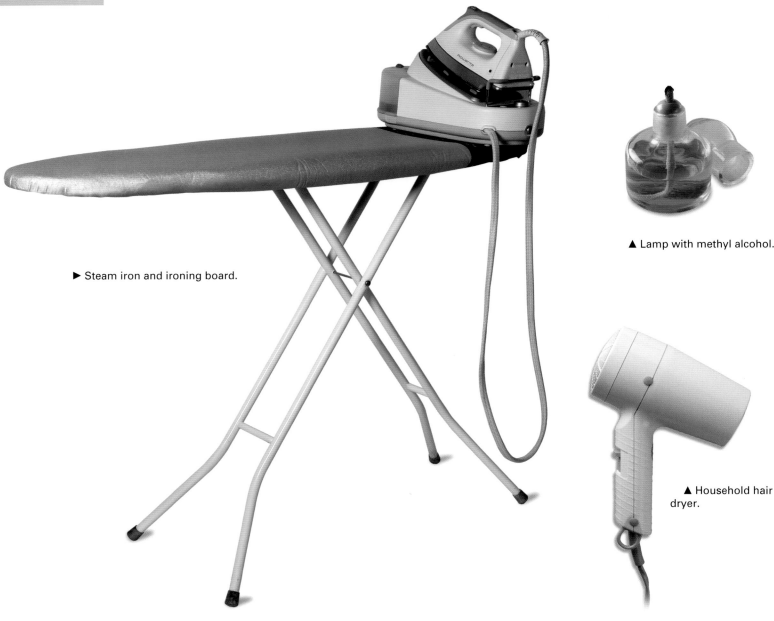

▶ Steam iron and ironing board.

▲ Lamp with methyl alcohol.

▲ Household hair dryer.

Different Types

Dryer

Household hair dryers are often used in the studio as an auxiliary tool for drying printing screens after they have been cleaned, and also for drying dyes and lacquers on fabrics that have been printed. The most powerful ones are best, with controls for airflow and temperature since it will sometimes be necessary to use cold air.

Iron and Ironing Board

The iron is used for removing wrinkles and smoothing fabrics that are to be printed. It is also used on the dye or paint on textiles that have already been printed to fix them with heat, in the devoré process to activate the

devoré mixture and begin the process, and in batik to eliminate the wax. The best irons for use in the studio are those that have an external water supply, although it is also possible to utilize normal household irons. In any case, they should have a control to regulate the flow of steam, since sometimes the iron should be used without it.

Containers

These are needed for the dying process. It is important to have a large collection of containers, preferably in clear plastic. Each one should be used for a specific color to avoid accidentally mixing tones. It is also very useful to have a selection of plastic containers

that can be reused. They can be used for mixing paint and pastes for printing. Plastic spoons should be used for mixing and applying printing pastes, while a wooden stirring stick should be used for mixing the components of screen-print emulsion and for stirring dyes.

Alcohol Lamp

Alcohol lamps are made of glass, and they are used for heating the wax that is used for making reserves in the batik technique. They are containers for methyl alcohol and have a lid, often made of ceramic that holds a wick with an end submerged in the alcohol. The top holds the wick in place, and its flame can

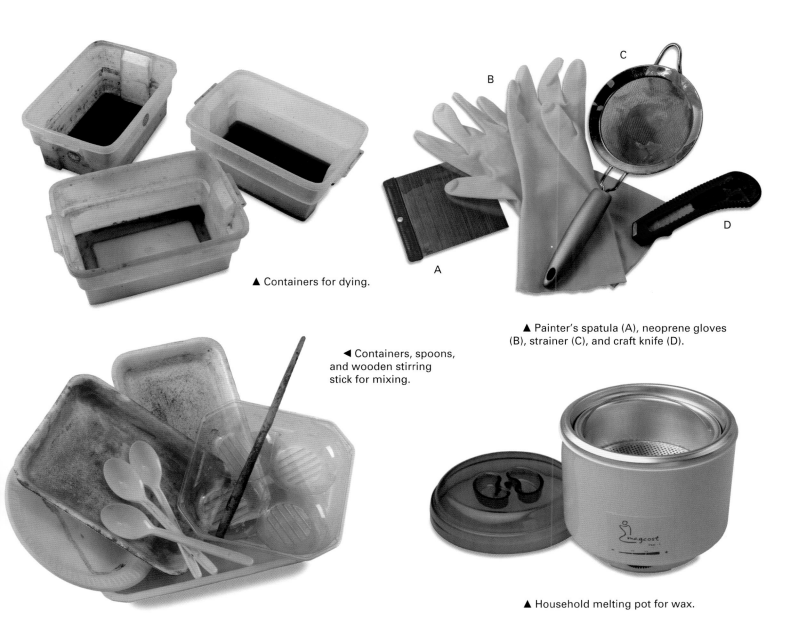

▲ Containers for dying.

◄ Containers, spoons, and wooden stirring stick for mixing.

▲ Painter's spatula (A), neoprene gloves (B), strainer (C), and craft knife (D).

▲ Household melting pot for wax.

be extinguished by replacing its glass cover. You must take some safety measures when working with this tool because methyl alcohol is highly flammable and toxic. Be very careful, and keep it away from other possible heat sources and flammable materials. It should be kept in a locked cupboard.

Melting Pot for Wax

Melting pots for wax that is used for cosmetic purposes can also be used for melting the wax used for making batik fabrics. They are less expensive than pots made for use with tjantings, and they are a good alternative to alcohol lamps, which require more safety measures.

Strainer

Kitchen strainers, along with an intermediary screen, are used for straining the wax used for batik prepared in the studio. They help eliminate any solid particles from the prepared wax.

Gloves

Neoprene gloves are indispensable for working with irritants like screen-printing emulsions, devoré paste, and bleach that might come into contact with the skin. Latex and polyethylene gloves only protect your hands from dyes, paints, and inks.

Craft Knife

A craft knife with refillable blades is very useful. It usually has a plastic handle, inside of which is a sharpened blade that can be removed and discarded at will. It is used for various cutting tasks.

Painter's Spatula

Painter's spatulas consist of a wide, flexible piece of metal with a narrow plastic handle on one side. It is mainly used in painting for applying pastes and putty and for leveling large surfaces. In the printing studio it is used in the batik process for scraping and removing built up wax.

The Studio

Space and Organizing the Studio

The textile printing studio must be well organized and kept in order. It is best to have a large space that is well ventilated and has natural light, if possible. It is generally better if it can be on a ground floor, and at the end of the street, which makes it easier for getting materials in and out. It is also helpful to have some space outdoors for hanging the fabrics. The size and distribution of the studio will depend on the techniques that are employed and the number of people that work in it. In any case, the interior should be large enough for comfortably carrying out the work, with room to move around and storage for the products, materials, and finished pieces.

It should have different areas for working on the different tasks, as well as several areas for storage: one for keeping fabrics, another for storing the supplies, and a third for keeping the works and textiles after they have been finished. In addition, an area for printing work, another area for the dying process, and a washing area with a sink and a washing machine is needed. It is also a good idea to have a space for doing design work. A special space, separate from the studio, will be helpful for the preparatory tasks required for serigraphy.

The studio should be well illuminated with even, general lighting. Fluorescent tubes are recommended, with task lighting available as required in several areas.

The work surfaces should be sufficient for carrying out the typical work, and there should be enough printing tables for doing the job correctly; they should be large, of the correct height, and covered so the surface is soft but durable. You can use foam rubber and felt, for example. In addition, there should be special printing tables for doing T-shirts, a surface for a printing press if it is a tabletop model, or work tables for batik and serti stretchers, for example.

The heat should be kept low in the winter to keep some of the products from drying, but high enough for working comfortably. There should be enough air vents in the entire studio.

There should be a separate room with a lock for serigraphy. It should be a dust-free environment that can be completely darkened. It should have a double illumination system with separate switches: one for normal lighting and the other with yellow incandescent light bulbs. This space should also be divided into different areas for the different processes: one for working with emulsion, another for light exposure, an area with a large sink and a hose for washing the screens, and a storage area for the finished screens.

▼ The studio should have ample space and natural light. There should be several tables for carrying out the different printing processes, an area for ironing, and a place for storing the fabrics.

Safety

Dangerous products must be stored separately, inside a metal locker with a lock, if possible, and far from sources of heat. All containers should be tightly sealed to avoid evaporation, and they should be arranged so that their toxicity warnings are visible upon opening the locker. Heat sources like hot plates, alcohol lamps, and electric tjantings should be kept away from the flammable products. All studios should have fire extinguishers of the required type and size for the studio. They should be visible, easily accessible, and inspected regularly. There should also be a first aid kit that is easily accessible. In addition, it is a good idea to have emergency phone numbers within view, perhaps near the telephone. It is important to keep a file with the technical and safety sheets for all the hazardous materials, so you can consult them at any time in case of doubt or in time of emergency. It would not be overdoing it to put a poster on the wall with the danger symbols and their meanings, and the precautions that should be taken.

Leftover products should be disposed of according to the local regulations. They

▲ It is a good idea to have a large, sturdy ladder to access the steamer.

should never be discarded because they can contaminate the environment. It is very important to be familiar with the regulations regarding dangerous substances, and to be aware of whether there is a schedule for picking them up or if they must be taken to a nearby landfill or treatment plant. The washing area should have a collection system for residual water according to the specific environmental regulations of your area.

► There should be one area for dyeing work, and another for washing that has a sink and a washing machine.

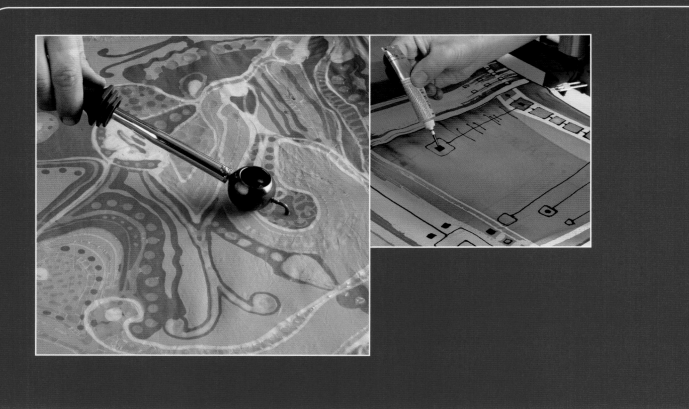

In this chapter we will explain in detail the principal techniques of printing textiles by impression and reserve. The techniques of impression include block printing and serigraphy, and the reserve techniques are batik and serti. We will demonstrate the fundamentals of each process, from the preparation work and preliminary aspects to the numerous possibilities that they offer. The chapter begins with a section on the preliminary aspects dedicated to patterns and color, followed by detailed information about the printing techniques. It also offers a full explanation of the bleaching and devoré techniques. Finally, we will explain the processes of the reserve techniques. We will begin with the technical processes that every person who wishes to practice this discipline must learn, and go on to the most complicated processes that more experienced craftsmen can find and adapt approaches that will help them develop and enrich their work.

Technical Processes

Preliminary Aspects

Creating printed designs on textiles requires, in most cases, a design. It is possible to begin printing directly, without a previous design, where the immediacy and spontaneity will be of primary value. In this sense, working directly offers a large field of investigation and creativity. However, the majority of textile work requires a previous design.

Design is the application of the thinking that is required for any creation, before beginning any process, and it becomes indispensable because it supposes an analysis of the ideas. Thus, it serves to deepen the initial concept, allows it to evolve, and becomes an ally in the exploration of solutions of form and color. It helps you think about the motif of the print, visualize it, and convert it into a powerful aid in the creative process.

The design will depend on the chosen printing technique, and at the same time it will be directly conditioned by it. Design and technique form part of the global process of creation. The designs can range from simple sketches to very detailed and colorful projects. In this sense, it is important to point out the use of new technologies in the process, such as digital images and the use of computers. The possibilities of form and color are endless; numerous resources can be used as a source of inspiration when creating originals as well as for creating forms directly on the computer.

You must also decide what printing approach you will take, that is, if it will be a single image or a pattern. The single image will be a motif printed with specific and careful placement, while a printed pattern is a motif that is repeated following a predetermined sequence that will extend across the entire textile. Creating patterned fabrics requires careful design work as we will explain next.

Motif

The motif is the basic module of the repeated design for creating the textile, and the motif can be repeated in all directions on the fabric. It is based on a given design that, after a few steps, is reworked into a motif that can then be repeated in any direction to create a patterned print through the process of serigraphy. There are different approaches to creating this type of motif, depending on the original design. Here, we will demonstrate the method for creating the motif based on a design with no background. There are other methods of creating repeatable motifs for more complex designs, for example, if the original design has a background color. However, we will not go into them because they are outside the scope of this book. There are computer programs for creating such motifs, although they are mainly used in industry.

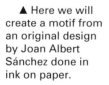
▲ Here we will create a motif from an original design by Joan Albert Sánchez done in ink on paper.

▲ **1.** The design is enlarged on a photocopier to achieve a composition with open forms that can be used to make the motif.

◄ **2.** The first step is to pull the design apart in the shape of a cross to establish vertical and horizontal axes. We are careful not to cut into any form.

▲ **3.** After the parts, or quarters, of the motif have been established, the upper ones are reversed with the lower ones, from right to left and left to right. Thus, quarter A moves to the lower right, B to the lower left, C to the upper right, and D to the upper left.

Creating the Motif

The motif is the reformulation of the design, adapting it so it can be reproduced in any direction. The adaptation of the forms requires a series of established steps that create a new motif derived from the original. The form of the resulting motif will differ from the original, but once the printing process is finished the results will look like the first design. After making the original design it is broken into four parts, establishing a vertical separation and a horizontal one. Separating the design into four quarters will always be done without damaging any of the forms; they will be cut through the background. Next, the placement of the shapes will be changed, moving the upper ones down, and the lower ones up, and the ones on the left to the right, and those on the right to the left. A certain amount of space must be left between them, and the motif is completed by adding designs that match the original one in the space. The shape or outline of the motif should be symmetrical. For example, if the lower part of the vertical separation sticks out, the upper part should have an indentation so they will fit exactly when the printing is done.

▲ **4.** A certain amount of space is left between the quarters, equal in both directions. In other words, the separation between quarters D and C of the vertical axis is the same as the separation between B and A, and that of D and B is the same as that of C and A. The free space in the axes can vary, but it must always be equal between them.

◄ **5.** The design is then completed, closing the unfinished shapes and creating new ones matching the original project.

◄ **6.** The finished motif.

Possible mistakes in the preparation of the motif appear during the printing process, and in this phase of the project they cannot be corrected. One of the typical problems is caused by asymmetry of the elements of the upper and lower, or left and right, sides of the same axis. This is when there is an element in the motif that does not show perfect symmetry in respect to a corresponding element on the other side of the motif.

▶ The asymmetry at one side of the axis of the motif in respect to the other side of the same axis has left an open space in the pattern.

▲ When this has been discovered it can be corrected by adding design elements before printing on the fabric.

Another Example of a Motif

Next, we will show another example of creating the motif and its practical application by screen-printing it on a fabric that will be used for the lining of an article of clothing. In this case, the motif is based on a closed design, joining the quarters without leaving separation between them and adding elements based on the original to unite the design of the four parts or quarters of the form.

▶ **1.** The motif will be based on an original design by Joan Albert Sánchez and Marian Piano in gouache on paper. The paper is divided into quarters, without cutting any of the forms, to establish a vertical axis and a horizontal axis.

▶ **2.** The quarters are arranged as we explained before: moving the upper ones down and the right side to the left, and vice versa, and attaching them to a paper support. In this case we have joined the two axes without leaving any free space. To avoid problems of blank space in the printing process, we have placed a dot at the intersection of the quarters on the left, and extended elements of the figures at the top right and bottom left of the lower right-hand quarter, so they occupy part of the adjacent quarters.

▲ 3. When the motif is finished, a photocopy is made on tracing paper at the required size, and the form is cut out.

▶ 4. It is then reproduced on the printing screen (see page 74).

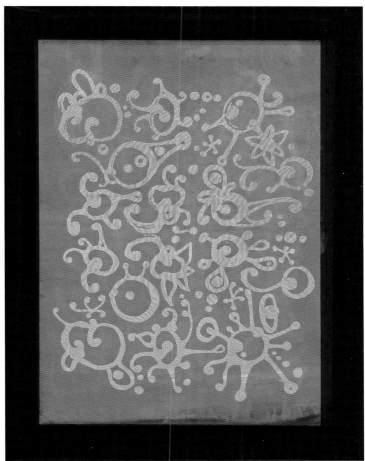

▼ 5. It is printed on the textile following the established pattern (see page 85).

Color

Another aspect implied in the design and posterior printing is color. Color is the chromatic sensation produced by light rays in the visual organs, that is, the sensation experienced by the retina when it receives light. Light is the visible part of electromagnetic radiation, which human beings perceive between the infrared and ultraviolet waves, between 760 and 400 nanometers (a unit of measure of the length of a wave). The radiation is propagated through undulating motion or waves, and colors are perceived according to the variations in the longitude of the waves. The colors arrive at the retina through the spectrum of radiation, or the spectrum of light reflected from an object, which allows us to perceive matter of a specific color.

There are three basic colors: magenta, cyan, and yellow, which are known as the primary colors. They are the basics, and they can be mixed to make all the other colors. However, primary colors cannot be made from mixing other colors. Mixing two primary colors makes a secondary color, and mixing a secondary color with a primary color creates a tertiary color. Every color has a complementary color. Black is the result of mixing the three primary colors. This is called synthesis, or the subtractive method of color. The pastes and dyes that are used for textile printing are mixed according to the subtractive method.

Here, we will show a practical example of the subtractive color method with the printing of a T-shirt, where you will see the creation of secondary colors from combinations of the three primaries. In this case we will use printing inks, although the use of the colors and their mixtures will be similar to all the pastes and dyes used in the different printing techniques, where only the application will vary according to the different processes. This exercise, done by Rosa Marín Martín Sol and based on typography by Laura Meseguer, illustrates the customary way of printing any T-shirt with the serigraphy technique. Here, you will see the method of printing with a motif (superimposing the motif).

◄ **1.** The design is created first. In this exercise we will print a lowercase "*a*" in the three alphabets that belong to the Rumba typographic family, designed by Laura Meseguer, with the three primary colors. The forms will be superimposed, each in a primary color, on a computer and printed on paper in the desired format.

▼ **2.** The design on paper is placed on the T-shirt, locating it exactly where it is to be printed. Using it as a template, the edges of the motif are marked with masking tape, which adheres to the knit fabric. The tape will serve as a printing guide for correctly placing the three letters.

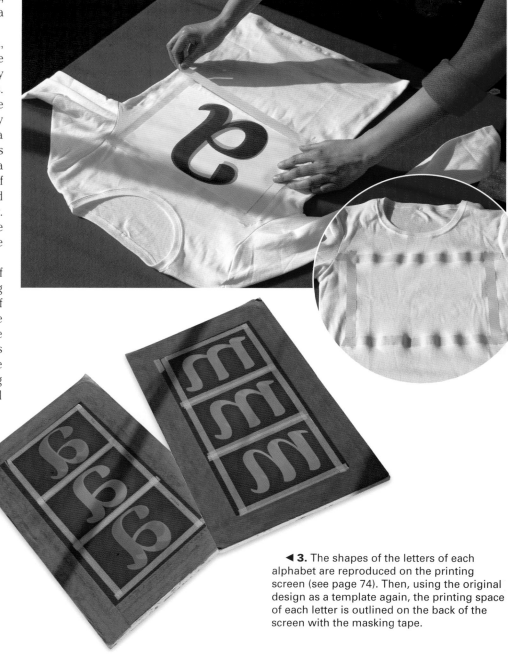

◄ **3.** The shapes of the letters of each alphabet are reproduced on the printing screen (see page 74). Then, using the original design as a template again, the printing space of each letter is outlined on the back of the screen with the masking tape.

◄ **4.** The cotton knit T-shirt is placed on the printing table with a sheet of cardboard, or lightweight cardboard as shown here, to protect the back in case the printing ink bleeds through the fabric.

► **5.** Mixing the primary colors by juxtaposition requires printing the lightest first, then the intermediate, and finally the darkest. First, we print the central letter with the lightest primary color, yellow. The screen is placed with the back in contact with the fabric and with the letter perfectly centered, paying close attention to lining up the four sides of masking tape on the screen with those on the T-shirt.

► **6.** The letters above and below are covered with newspaper fixed with masking tape to avoid accidents.

▲ **7.** A sufficient amount of yellow printing ink is deposited on the screen with a plastic spoon, forming a line that is as wide as the motif. The ink is always placed above the design.

▲ **8.** We print by dragging the ink toward us, applying light and even pressure with the squeegee; then we return in the opposite direction, toward the top of the letter. To remove the screen we very carefully lift one of the long sides until the design is released from the shirt.

▲ **10.** Next, we print the second primary color, magenta. The lower letter on the screen is centered according to the masking tape guides. Notice that this letter to be printed in magenta will be printed over the yellow in some areas, while in others the original yellow will stay the same.

▲ **9.** The result is a letter printed in the lightest primary color. It is then left to dry.

MIXING TWO PRIMARY COLORS

The mixture of two primary colors has created a secondary color, orange.

◄ **11.** As done previously, the central letter is protected with newspaper to avoid accidents. Then, the motif is printed in magenta. The screen is removed and the shirt is allowed to dry.

▲ **12.** Finally, we print the upper letter on the screen with the other primary color, cyan, which at the same time is the complementary color of orange. It is centered and the lower letter is protected with newspaper, and the ink is deposited on the screen above the letter.

▲ **13.** The letter is printed in cyan and left to dry.

MIXING CYAN WITH YELLOW AND MAGENTA

The three printed letters. The mixture of cyan with yellow and magenta has created the color black in the central part of the designs. The mixture of the primary colors yellow and blue have created the secondary color green in the left part of the motif; the complement of this is magenta, which is not in the mixture. Finally, the mixture of cyan and magenta have produced violet, which can be seen in some details of the letter, and their complement is yellow.

▲ **14.** The finished T-shirt.

PRINTING TECHNIQUES

*T*he impression techniques consist of printing the motif or motifs directly on the fabric. Impressions are made by transferring the design to the textile through pressure, and there are various techniques for doing this. The main ones are block printing and serigraphy, which are explained in full detail in this section.

We will also talk about others, like devoré and bleaching, although they can be considered approaches derived from these techniques, or a specialization of them. However, since they encompass a series of their own techniques and very specific methods, they deserve to be in a separate section.

Block Printing

Block printing is one of the easiest and least expensive techniques for printing a pattern on textiles. In essence, it is just a block that is used as a stamp for printing the design on the fabric. Blocks offer endless opportunities. The desired designs can be carved into linoleum, wood, or metal plates, although you can experiment with other common materials and elements. This approach lends itself to experimentation, since it combines the stamping process with the many possibilities of form and expression of the materials themselves. This highly versatile technique allows you to print a single image or very complex patterns that require the use of several blocks. The latter usually includes the use of various colors. However, this technique does not allow mass production of printed textiles since the outlines of the shapes, especially on wood and linoleum blocks, can lose their definition with heavy use. Planning the design becomes especially important because the stamped image is the mirror image of the block, so this should be kept in mind from the beginning. The colors used for printing should be somewhat thick, and there are special inks and paints for block printing.

▶ Carles de Roselló, 1990. Rayon crape skirt printed with several blocks, 35.5 inches (90 cm) long.

Traditionally, printing blocks have been made of wood, although metal molds attached to a wood base have been used for printing large runs, especially in Europe. The best woods for making printing blocks are those with close grains that are hard and durable, such as boxwood, beech, and sycamore, among others. However, creating blocks and seals with wood is very specialized work, requiring great skill in cutting the material. Wood carving is a complex artistic discipline that requires skillful handling of the chisels in making the cuts, and the ability to read the direction of the fibers and grain of the wood. Therefore, creating the blocks is far removed from printing with them, and they have traditionally been made by wood artists and wood-carvers.

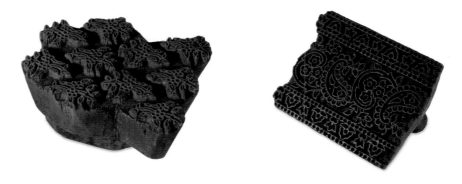

▲ Traditional Indian printing blocks carved from wood. In this case they are blocks for printing repeated patterns.

▶ **1.** Printing with several blocks allows the creation of multicolored textiles. In this image is an artisan working in Isfahan, Iran, stamping a shawl. He first positions the block on the fabric according to the design. He prints the fringe and the central design in red and blue, using different blocks for each motif and color. Then he prints the final detail in the central forms with indigo.

▶ **2.** He strikes the mold with his hand to print the entire design of the block on the fabric.

Creating Blocks with Linoleum

Nowadays, linoleum is being substituted for wood when making blocks in the studio. Linoleum is a widespread material; it is easy to find, not very expensive, very light, and sold in sheets of various sizes. It is homogenous, and unlike wood it has no grain, which makes it easy to work with. It is carved just like wood, cutting and removing the material with chisels made especially for linoleum. However, it does not require mastery of carving techniques, so it is possible to create complex shapes with just a little practice.

In essence, the technique consists of transferring a design onto the linoleum block with carbon paper and then carving the shapes by cutting with different chisels, outlining the design and removing the areas that are not to be printed. The linoleum should be attached to a wood support with a handle to make the process of printing on fabric easier. If you are printing repeating patterns with complex shapes or different colors, you should make several blocks, since large blocks are hard to handle and lead to defective or uneven impressions. The best blocks for the studio are those that you can use with one hand. The printing can be done by hand, following the traditional process, or you can use a printing press. Here, you can see some possible uses of linoleum in different examples by Rosa Oliveras.

◄ **1.** First, draw a full-size sketch of the motif on paper with a pencil. In this case, she is making a design vaguely inspired by ethnic forms, which will be used along with others (see the following sections) to print fabric that will be used to make a belt.

► **2.** The design is photocopied and the shapes that will be left in relief are filled in with a marker. This image will serve as a guide for cutting the linoleum.

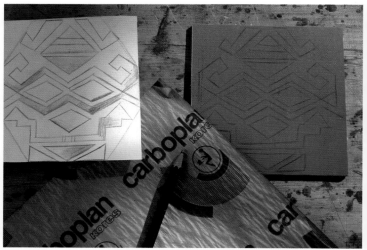

▲ **3.** The linoleum block is measured and marked at the desired size, in this case 5.5 by 5.5 inches (14 by 14 cm). Using a metal ruler as a guide, the linoleum is cut with a straight blade or a craft knife. The cut starts at the top and moves toward the artist.

▲ **4.** The design is transferred to the surface of the linoleum block. The carbon paper is laid on the block and the paper with the design is placed over it, aligning it carefully with the linoleum, and the motif is transferred by retracing the pencil lines.

◄ **5.** Begin cutting the linoleum, using the design colored with the marker as a guide. First, cut the outline of the design, following the lines with a v-shaped chisel. Always cut away from your body, with your free hand (which should hold the linoleum) behind the area that you are carving to avoid any accidents.

▲ **6.** Work by zones; after one part is outlined, remove the material inside using a chisel, or gouge, with a u-shaped blade.

▲ **7.** Continue working by zones, cutting the outline and then clearing it out.

▶ **8.** When you have finished cutting, and before printing the fabric, make a proof. It will let you see that the block matches the design, and you will see possible problems or mistakes, if there are any. Apply an even coat of printing ink to the block with a foam roller.

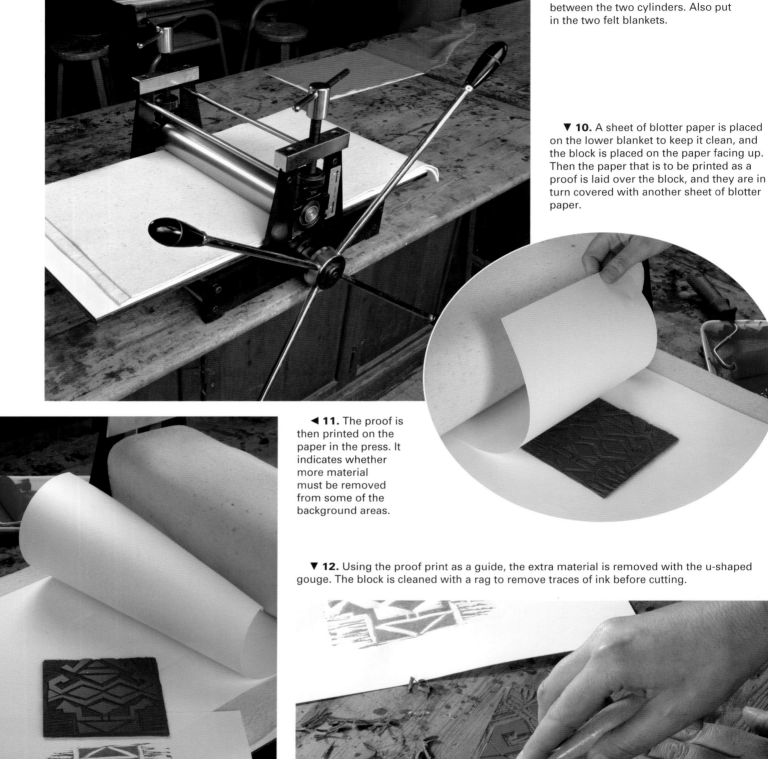

◄ **9.** Place the platen on the press, between the two cylinders. Also put in the two felt blankets.

▼ **10.** A sheet of blotter paper is placed on the lower blanket to keep it clean, and the block is placed on the paper facing up. Then the paper that is to be printed as a proof is laid over the block, and they are in turn covered with another sheet of blotter paper.

◄ **11.** The proof is then printed on the paper in the press. It indicates whether more material must be removed from some of the background areas.

▼ **12.** Using the proof print as a guide, the extra material is removed with the u-shaped gouge. The block is cleaned with a rag to remove traces of ink before cutting.

The textile can be printed by hand or with the help of a press. It is used for printing stand-alone designs that require a good, clear impression. The platen is placed on the lower cylinder with one of the felt blankets on it, then blotter paper is added to keep the blanket clean, and the fabric that you wish to print is added. The block is then laid in the desired position on the fabric and is covered with another sheet of blotter paper and a felt blanket. After they are all between the two cylinders, lower both ends of the upper cylinder simultaneously, leveling them using the scale marked on the frame and adjusting them until they are applying light pressure to the printing block. Start to print by turning the spokes of the press. The block will pass between the cylinders, making an impression of the block on the fabric. It is important to adjust the pressure correctly; if it is not enough the design will be uneven with tonal variations, and if it is too much it can damage the press. It is a good idea to run some tests on pieces of fabric similar to the one being printed to correctly adjust the pressure.

► **1.** Apply an even coat of printing ink with a foam roller. Roll it in all directions without pressing too hard on the linoleum block. Completely cover the entire design with an even layer, avoiding the buildup of too much ink in some places.

▲ **2.** Put the fabric (cotton taffeta) on the blotter paper that is on the blanket, which is on the platen. Next, place the block in the desired position, in this case at one end of the piece of fabric. Cover it with a new blotter paper and another felt blanket, and then run it through the press.

◄ **3.** The result is an impression of the design.

Hand Printing

Hand printing is the quickest and most comfortable method of printing blocks. When the block is placed in the desired position on the fabric, it is pressed firmly or struck a single time using a mallet with a nylon or rubber head. The pressure must be uniform to create a clean and precise impression, otherwise the printed image will be irregular.

In this section we demonstrate the hand printing method, explaining how to make a pattern using several blocks. In this case, we begin with two previously made blocks and create a design for a new block to complement the others. Remember that you must allow each one of the images to dry before printing the next one.

▲ 1. We begin with two existing blocks, made from linoleum mounted on wood by Elisa Rubió.

Samples of the two blocks are printed on paper to serve as guides for making the new block, and to establish a possible composition for the print.

◄ 2. The design is developed based on the two previously made blocks, progressing as shown in this sequence. First the general form or outline of the block is established, which here will be octagonal, relating it to the other blocks. Next, the design is drawn in pencil, creating the central motif of the composition, two diamonds framed by an upper and lower zigzag border. This first sketch is modified by adding new geometric elements above and below. Then, the changes are evaluated, and some elements are changed back to the way they were and some new ones are added. Finally, the definitive design is rendered in pencil to serve as a model for making the block.

► 3. After the linoleum block is finished, it is glued to a wood support (here, a piece of plywood with a melamine veneer) with contact cement. When it has completely dried a handle is screwed to the back.

▼ 4. Linoleum blocks can also be glued to a piece of wood that is cut to match the outline of the motif, and a wood handle is added.

► 5. Apply an even layer of printing ink on the block with a foam roller. The ink is applied in all directions without applying too much pressure, gripping the roller lightly. Then the block is placed carefully on the fabric in the desired position, in the center of the fabric lined up with the other impressions. Firm pressure is applied with both hands since it is a long block.

Typographic designs constitute a special case. Remember that the printed impression is the reverse image of the original design. They are symmetrical in the same way that an object is related to its image in the mirror: elements that are at the right of the composition on the block will appear at the left in the print. This requires careful planning of the design motifs, and it is a fundamental issue when it comes to typographic images. The letters or words must be created as reversed images when the block is carved so that they will read correctly when they are printed. Here, we show an example of this as well as a simple method for making blocks with typographic characters.

▲ **1.** First, the desired word is designed. Here, it will act as a header for the previous print.

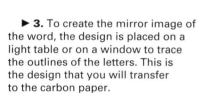

◄ **2.** When the design is finished, a full-size image is drawn in ink on paper.

► **3.** To create the mirror image of the word, the design is placed on a light table or on a window to trace the outlines of the letters. This is the design that you will transfer to the carbon paper.

◄ **4.** The design is transferred to the linoleum and is then carved. On the proof prints you can see how the image of the word is reversed when it is printed.

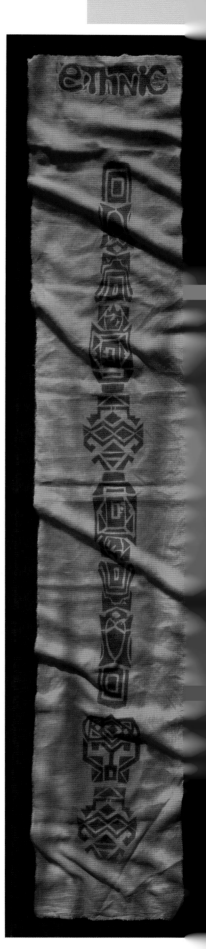

► **5.** Here is the fabric after printing.

Other Techniques

It is possible to use materials other than wood and linoleum for printing designs on textiles. There is a great number of materials such as erasers, expanded polystyrene (EPS), natural and synthetic sponges, packing foam, and cork. Erasers and cork can be carved with a sharp knife or a craft knife, using a technique similar to that for wood. Special cutters are used for EPS, and for some packing foam,

although in some cases serrated knives can be used. Nevertheless, craft knives and sharpened knives are mainly used for creating specific effects, like rough outlines or certain textures.

Other approaches to printing are based on using everyday objects, pieces of machinery, and vegetables.

PRINTING WITH OBJECTS

One of the most interesting approaches to direct printing on textiles is the use of objects. All kinds of elements can be used to make the impression, such as metal or plastic parts of machinery, electrical parts of machinery, objects from around the house, etc. There is a wide range of possibilities, only limited by your own creativity. Here, we illustrate some designs printed in ink as examples.

Bubble Wrap 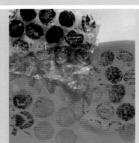	Packaging with cells filled with air can be used as a stamp to make spots and gradations	
Printing with Containers 	Containers offer many possibilities. In this case, we used the lid of a bottle to print circular shapes.	
	Here, we used the ring from common adhesive tape.	
Printing with String 	String or wire rolled around something or attached to a board can create a multitude of shapes.	
Printing with Household Items 	Objects that are commonly used at home can also be used for textile printing. The end of a clothespin can be used to create lines.	

Printing With Machine Parts 	This metal piece from a machine was used to print circular elements.	
	Plastic parts from appliances can easily be used to print shapes.	
A Combination of Prints 	It is possible to create very original prints using a combination of different pieces and colors.	
Printing with Electrical Parts 	A connector for electric wires was used to make this print. A different shape can be printed with each side.	

CREATING TEXTURES

Block printing also offers the possibility of creating textures. The texture is printed by making an impression on fabric with a block over a support that transmits its texture. To do this put the fabric, which should be very thin, on the textured support and then print it with the block or piece with the desired color. Here are some examples of prints with textures.

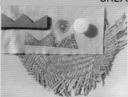

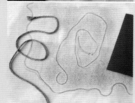

Very thin cotton taffeta was printed on a base of woven straw with a linoleum block and printing ink.

Here, the same fabric was printed with the same block and printing ink. The support was a piece of perforated felt. The texture and the design on the felt were imprinted on the fabric.

You can achieve interesting effects by placing objects between the printing table and the fabric. Here, a silk taffeta scarf was printed by placing a piece of wool string under it and then printing the surface of the fabric with an uncarved linoleum block, a small amount of printing ink, and light pressure. The result is the impression of the texture and sinuous shape of the string on the fabric.

PRINTING WITH VEGETABLES

Vegetables and plants are certainly one of the best-known and most widespread resources for printing on textiles. Printing ink or paint can be directly applied to leaves and flowers that have been pressed and dried and then printed on fabric. It is also possible to use different kinds of vegetables and their leaves, as we explain here.

▲ **1.** Artichokes are the flowering parts of the plant (*cynara scolymus*), and are formed of many leaves. Cutting the vegetable longitudinally reveals the most interesting shapes.

▲ **2.** Since artichoke leaves are very durable, they can be used fresh. For printing, ink is applied evenly with a foam roller in all directions while pressing lightly.

▲ **3.** First, the excess ink is removed with a sheet of newspaper, and some tests are made on paper to evaluate the shape and resolution of the impression before printing on the fabric.

▲ **4.** Print the fabric, in this case cotton taffeta, using the test sheet as a guide. Here, as the motif is printed it is turned, thus creating a rhythmic repetition.

▲ **5.** Here is the printed fabric.

▲ **1.** It is also possible to make impressions with heads of cabbage (*brassica oleracea*), by cutting them in half.

▲ **2.** Printing ink is applied on the cut side and applied directly to the fabric.

▶ **3.** This is the printed cotton taffeta.

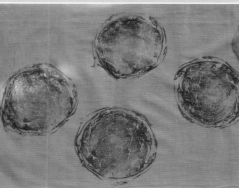

Serigraphy

Serigraphy is a very versatile printing process. It consists of a screen made of a frame that serves as a support for a mesh, which has closed areas and open areas with the image that is to be printed. The print is made by pushing the printing ink through the screen that is in contact with the fabric with a squeegee. The ink only passes through the open areas and stays on the screen in the closed areas, resulting in an image printed on the fabric. This technique, also known as screen printing or silk screening, is thought to be a derivation of the traditional stenciling process. The name is derived from the French *sérigraphe*, which itself is an abbreviated form of *séricigraphe*, which comes from the Latin *sericum*, which means "silk" (before the arrival of synthetic fibers the mesh was made of that material), and the French *graphie*, which is "graph."

Serigraphy is a specialized printing system but is technically inexpensive, which makes it easy to create any kind of motif, from the simplest to the most complex such as photographic reproductions. It lets you reproduce a design with any amount of detail a great number of times. This makes it the best technique for mass producing printed items like T-shirts. Here, we will demonstrate the entire process of creating screen-printed designs done by Miriam Albiñana and Joan Albert Sánchez.

► Mónica Pérez Sierra, 2007. Screen-printed cotton knit shirt and pants, 24.5 × 15.5 inches (60 × 39 cm) (shirt), 25.25 × 28 inches (64 × 71 cm) (pants).

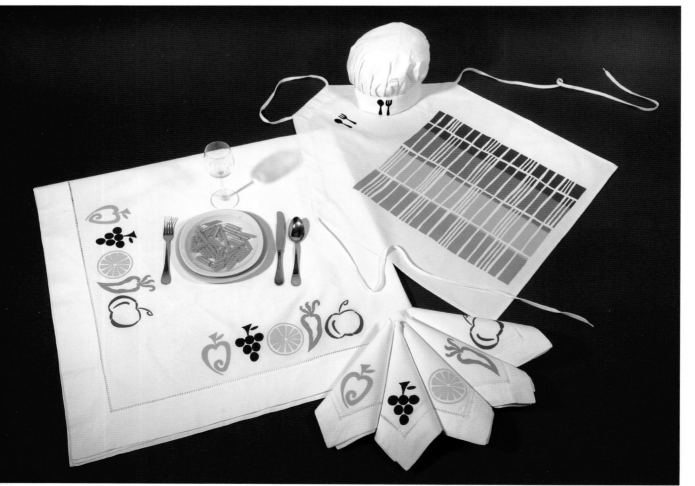

◄ Laura Muniesa, 2006. Corporate identity project for a restaurant: tablecloth, apron, and chef's toque. Five-color screen print on cotton.

Making the Screen

The screen is the key to a successful serigraphic print. Although screens can be purchased ready-made, it is possible to make your own in the studio. This not only lowers your cost, but it allows you to control every phase of the project. The screen should be made with a strong wood frame with thick wood sides that are joined with tenons at the corners. Stretchers for painting canvases can also be used and are not too expensive. The best mesh is made of polyester because it is very stable and resistant to water. For normal printing you would usually use mesh measuring 125 threads per inch (48 per cm), but you can use others like 90 threads per inch (36 per cm) for metallic inks or 196 threads per inch (75 per cm) if you require

better resolution. The latter is similar to the finest silk fabric screens. Here, we will demonstrate the process of making a screen that will serve for any serigraphic printing task.

► **1.** Wood frames are best for making printing screens in the studio because they are inexpensive and can be reused. In this case, we will make the screen with a square frame.

◄ **2.** First, a coat of acrylic paint is applied, completely covering the entire surface of the frame, and then it is left to dry. This will protect the wood, waterproofing it as much as possible to keep it from warping and damaging the screen when it comes into contact with water and other products.

▼ **3.** The mesh is chosen based on the project it will be used for, and it is attached to the frame. This mesh is a voile fabric.

◄ **4.** It is laid on the frame with about 1 inch (2 cm) hanging over the side. We attach it at one corner with two staples placed diagonally so the mesh will not tear when it is pulled tight.

▲ **5.** The mesh is pulled tightly with the threads parallel to the sides of the frame, then the opposite corner is stapled in the same manner as before.

▲ **6.** The operation is repeated on the third corner of the frame.

▶ **7.** Next, the sides between the attached corners are stapled, starting from the first corner to the second, placing the staples diagonally at regular intervals. Then begin at the first corner and move toward the third, again making the staples diagonal, but in the opposite direction. Make sure that the threads stay parallel to the sides.

▼ **8.** The extra fabric is cut off with sharp scissors following the threads of the mesh, leaving about 1 inch (2 cm) hanging over the side of the frame.

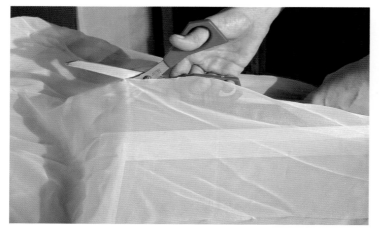

▶ **9.** The mesh is pulled and aligned, and the last corner is stapled. Then the screen must be tightened.

► **10.** It is very helpful to have a pair of canvas stretching pliers for tightening the mesh. The frame is placed at the edge of the work surface so that one side hangs over slightly, and a weight is set on the opposite side to keep it from moving. The edge of the mesh is grasped with the pliers and pulled down to tighten it. The mesh is stapled to the wood with the other hand; the staples should be diagonal and in the opposite direction then the row across from them. The process is repeated on the other side.

▼ **11.** Make sure the staples are all the way in the wood by tapping them with a hammer.

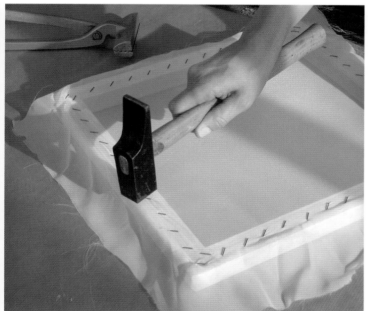

▲ **12.** The excess mesh is then cut off, leaving just a small amount around the outside of the frame.

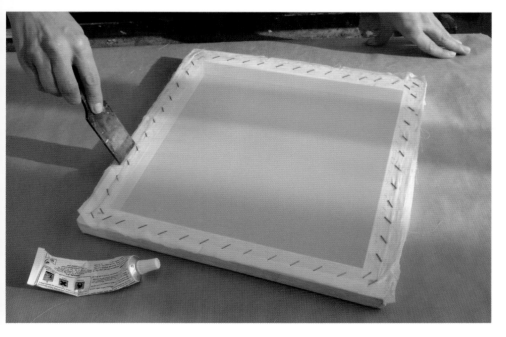

◄ **13.** Finally, a coating of contact cement is applied over the stapled areas with a spatula, and then it is allowed to dry completely. The cement helps to hold the screen and waterproofs it, protecting the staples from rusting. Do not allow any glue to get on the mesh within the frame because it will seal it and cause problems.

Emulsion

After the print screen is properly constructed, the design can be applied to it by different processes. The most widely used process is photo emulsion, although it is also possible to make reserves directly on the screen with different materials such as wax, paint, white glue, paper, and self-adhesive plastic (see page 92). Photo emulsion is a technical process requiring a light-sensitive emulsion, an original, and equipment for exposing the screen to light. The first step consists of applying the emulsion to the mesh. This process is always done in a dust-free room separated from the studio that can be darkened completely and that has yellow lighting. The emulsion is prepared following the manufacturer's instructions as printed on the packaging, then it is applied with a squeegee used for emulsion only. A small amount of emulsion is placed at the top of the screen and spread up and down and back and forth (if the screen is large), alternating on both sides of the mesh with the squeegee. The last pass should be made on the inside of the screen, so that the thicker and more homogenous layer comes into contact with the original in the exposure process. The objective is to cover the mesh with a very thin layer of emulsion that is as homogenous as possible, which you can check by looking at it against the light. During the application you should avoid vibrations and changes in pressure, speed, and the angle of the squeegee. You should also avoid getting emulsion on the frame, since it can later peel off and cause problems.

▲ **1.** Prepare the photo emulsion in a separate space from the studio that has yellow lighting. Here, the emulsion is being mixed with a liquid sensitizer. Wear protective gloves when pouring the sensitizer into the container of emulsion.

▲ **2.** The two ingredients are mixed with a glass or wood stirrer (never metal, which would react with the emulsion); then it is left to rest until the bubbles completely disappear (see the time indicated by the manufacturer).

▶ **3.** A small amount of emulsion is poured onto one end of the bottom of the screen and spread with a squeegee without pressing too hard.

▼ **4.** The squeegee is passed across the other side of the screen until it is uniform.

▲ **5.** Finally, the screen is left to dry horizontally with the bottom up for twenty-four hours in a dark place, like the emulsion room.

The photo emulsion technique is used to transfer a design onto the printing screen by hardening the photosensitive emulsion by exposing it to ultraviolet light. This technique includes several processes. First, the bottom of the screen is placed in contact with the design, which can be on acetate or tracing paper, although in some cases it can be an original. Next, it is exposed on an exposure table with a light source that has a high content of ultraviolet rays. These rays go through the transparent parts of the original or the design and cause the emulsion to harden by a chemical process. Then, the screen is rinsed with water. This causes the areas of the design that have remained covered and have not received any ultraviolet rays to wash out of the screen because they have not hardened. This way, you get a copy of the design on the screen, which can later be printed on the fabric.

◄ 1. The screen will be exposed with an original design based on vegetable elements, olive branches and acacia seeds, and spaghetti. They will be glued with white glue to a sheet of tracing paper after the composition is arranged.

One basic aspect is the amount of time that the mesh with the emulsion is exposed to the light on the exposure table. A correct amount of exposure time will result in a screen that is durable and has well-defined shapes. On the other hand, if it has been exposed to the light too long or not long enough, there can be problems with durability or the emulsion can block the screen. In industrial applications there are different methods for calculating the optimal exposure times, but in the studio it is best to follow the manufacturer's technical specifications, referring to the times for a specific light source of a determined brightness.

▲ 2. When the glue is completely dry, the original is placed in the center of the exposure table, with the paper on the glass with the objects up and the yellow light on.

▲ 3. The printing screen with the dry emulsion is placed with the bottom on the original and perfectly centered. Then the chain is laid across the screen, being very careful not to move it. The chain ensures that the rubber sheet will adapt correctly to the screen when the vacuum is turned on.

MAKING AN EXPOSURE TABLE IN THE STUDIO

Vacuum exposure tables can be substituted with other systems in the studio. One of the most common is a tabletop exposure unit made of wood parts, like a recycled box, for example, inside of which are mounted a number of fluorescent tubes that emit ultraviolet (UV) light. A sheet of glass is attached on top, where the original and the screen will be placed, covered with a thick, black rubber sheet to keep the light from escaping. On that is placed a board with weights to make sure it lies tightly against the screen.

Halogen lights can also be used to expose the screens. In this case, the original is put on a sheet of glass with the screen on top of it. Then they are placed on two easels, and the light bulb is laid on the floor underneath the screen. The top of the screen is covered much like the previous case, with rubber and weights.

A variation of this system is to put the original and the screen on dark rubber or Styrofoam, with a sheet of black paper on top directly on the floor, with a sheet of glass on top, and attach the halogen bulb to a structure (like a stick suspended between two easels) above them.

The distance from the light or lights to the screen should always be at least equal to the diagonal (corner to opposite corner) measure of the screen being exposed.

▶ **4.** The upper cover, with its rubber blanket, is closed and locked with the front clips. The yellow light is turned off and the suction pump is turned on. After the vacuum is established, the correct time is selected and the exposure begins. After the correct amount of time has passed, the UV lights are turned off and the screen is removed.

▼ **5.** Next, the screen is revealed, removing the emulsion from the areas that have not hardened. The screen is placed in the sink and washed with abundant cold water from a hose on both sides. The emulsion that did not harden is dissolved in the water; the areas of the design with open mesh appear, while the rest of the closed mesh with the hardened emulsion has a pink tone.

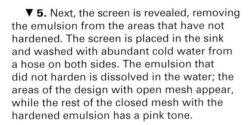

◀ **6.** The screen should be completely dry before being used. It can be air dried, or the process can be accelerated by using a hair dryer set on cool. Hot air should never be used since the polyester fibers could shrink and ruin the mesh and the screen. Try not to touch the emulsion until it is completely dry.

▶ **7.** The area where the mesh meets the frame is covered with gummed paper tape to keep it from staining the fabric during the printing process. The gummed side of the tape, previously dampened with water, is placed so that part is on the frame and part is on the mesh. Then it is allowed to dry.

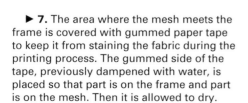

▶ **8.** This technique allows you to directly apply the emulsion to create specific shapes and effects. Here, we paint the shape of a seed directly on the screen to suggest the volume of the elements. Then it is left to dry in the sun.

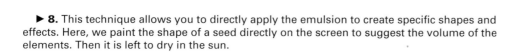

SCREEN DEFECTS

General Problems	Causes	Minor Problems in a Correctly Made Screen
Difficulty in spreading the emulsion on the screen. The emulsion does not adhere well to the mesh. Double images from the screen moving too much under the pressure of the squeegee during printing. Blurred reproduction. Fragility of the emulsion because the mesh gives too much during the printing, causing the appearance of pores and cracking in the emulsion.	Incorrect tightening of the mesh during construction of the printing screen.	Closed pores in some parts of the mesh after being developed. This problem is resolved by opening the pores with a very fine needle.
Bubbles in the emulsion that appear during the developing process.	Exposure time is too short. Dirty mesh.	Emulsion coming off from accidentally touching it with your hands before it was completely dry.
The emulsion disappears during the developing process.	Exposure time is too short. Incorrect preparation of the emulsion with an incorrect proportion of sensitizer. Use of an exposure table with inadequate lighting.	The emulsion was not completely dry and came off at one of the corners of the screen when you were applying the gummed paper tape. The solution consists of applying adhesive tape over the top of the screen to block the mesh.
After the screen is developed, a "veil" appears, a layer of traces of the unhardened emulsion diluted in water deposited on the screen.	Insufficient rinsing. This can be avoided by carefully rinsing the screen on both sides and leaving it to dry between sheets of newspaper.	Unclosed pores in the emulsion caused by the presence of dust on the glass of the exposure table.
Poorly defined image after the developing process.	Exposure time is too short. Emulsion layer is too thick. Poor contact between the screen and the original or the design. Emulsion in a poor state, past expiration date. Little contrast in the original, with not enough opacity.	The pore in the mesh is blocked with a drop of white glue. Let it dry completely before making any prints.

Printing

The print is made by placing the screen in the desired position: the bottom is in contact with the fabric, which has been smoothed and attached to the work surface with pins or spray tack adhesive. A line of printing ink is placed on the top of the screen, above the image or along one side of it, on an area where the emulsion is hardened (closed mesh). The ink is spread with a squeegee held at about 45 degrees, and pressure is applied as it is dragged over the image. The squeegee should be a little wider than the image and dragged across the screen gently while applying uniform pressure. In most cases it will be necessary to make another pass to achieve a good impression. This can be done by returning the squeegee to the starting point and making another pass in the same direction, or by beginning at the end point of the first pass and moving in the opposite direction. This will depend on your experience and personal preference.

After making the impression, the screen should be carefully lifted starting with one side, and it will pull away from the fabric. If you wish to make just a single print, the screen can be washed with abundant cold water to remove any ink residue. Remember that it is impossible to remove after the ink has dried, and it can obstruct the mesh and ruin the screen. If you are going to make another impression it is a good idea not to waste much time between each one.

Although the serigraphy technique does not have any particular difficulties, it is important to run some tests beforehand until you master the process. It is also a good idea to make some tests with the screen you plan to use before printing the chosen fabric to ascertain the amount of ink that is needed, the number of passes for achieving a clear image, and, if necessary, discover flaws in the screen.

Next, we will demonstrate a method for printing any motif on fabric, showing the process of printing a design using more than one color.

Holding the Screen

The screen should always be held perfectly still during the printing process to keep it from moving and causing blurring and double images. If necessary, a very large or heavy printing screen may require the help of another person to hold it while the printing is done. It is also possible to use different methods to attach the screen to the table or printing surface, like the printing arm for printing T-shirts (see page 45).

◀ **1.** The printing ink must be prepared before starting to print. We will use three colors, orange, light green, and dark green made from mixing various colors. Each will be made from a printing base paste. A sufficient quantity of the base for printing the design is placed in a tray, and small amounts of color ink are mixed with it to create the desired tone. This way, just the right amount of ink is made for printing, reducing the cost.

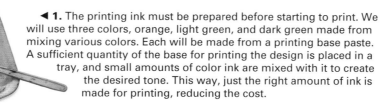

▲ **2.** After the three colors are mixed, the ink is placed on the top of the screen with plastic spoons. Here, the colors will be printed horizontally, so they are arranged in a line at one side of the composition on a closed area of the mesh without coming into contact with the motif. The colors are placed so they do not come into contact with each other.

▲ **3.** The printing screen is placed on the fabric (cotton twill) in the desired position. The screen is held firmly with one hand pressing on the frame, while the other hand controls the squeegee. The ink is spread with a continuous motion, putting uniform pressure on the squeegee, which is angled at 45 degrees.

▶ **4.** The screen is carefully lifted from one side until the fabric pulls away. The result of this first impression is a printed design with three defined colors that slightly mix with each other where they meet.

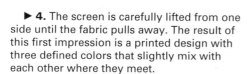

▶ ▶ **5.** In successive impressions the colors slowly mix together to create interesting gradated effects.

One of the advantages of serigraphy is the possibility of printing a single motif or creating a piece with a repeated pattern. By single motif we mean one or several forms printed in a specific place on the fabric, for example, a design on the front of a T-shirt. The motifs can be monochromatic, or they can be made with various colors. The latter requires deconstructing the design, creating several printing screens, and printing several times to create superimposed impressions or a group of colored motifs. Here, we explain the system for printing a single design by superimposing motifs created by Joan Albert Sánchez. Superimposing impressions requires designing two originals and then making a printing screen for each of them. The first impression, which will create the background motif, is done with printing lacquer; the second, which will be the superimposed motif, will be printed with relief ink. The modern motifs he has chosen contrast with the traditional Catalan checkered cotton taffeta that is used for making scarves.

◀ **1.** The fabric is laid on the printing table and is fixed with a tack adhesive spray. The first step consists of printing the background design, which is larger than the design that will be printed over it. The screen is placed with the bottom in contact with the fabric and properly positioned, carefully lined up with respect to the checkered pattern. Next, the lacquer, a light rose color that goes well with the fabric, is placed at the upper part of the screen. This paste is less fluid than the inks, so it will be necessary to use a larger amount to make the print.

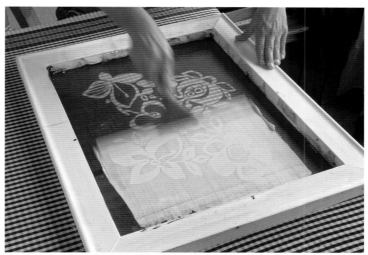

◀ **2.** The screen is held firmly to keep it from moving, and the lacquer is spread once with a continuous motion, holding the squeegee at 45 degrees. The impression is made with a single pass, because more could cause too much paste to build up on the fabric.

◀ **3.** The screen is very carefully lifted from one long side, and the fabric pulls away and is allowed to dry. To accelerate the drying you can use a hair dryer set on cool.

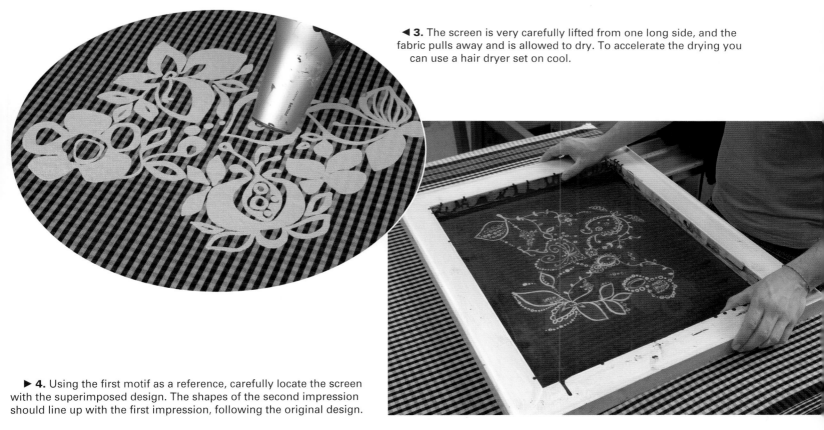

▶ **4.** Using the first motif as a reference, carefully locate the screen with the superimposed design. The shapes of the second impression should line up with the first impression, following the original design.

▲ **5.** It is printed with black relief ink. The impression is made with a single pass to avoid building up too much ink on the fabric.

▲ **6.** The screen is lifted carefully and the fabric pulls away. The second motif has been superimposed on the first one. It is left to dry according to the manufacturer's dircections.

► **7.** After it is dry, the fabric is placed face down on a clean white cloth and ironed for one to three minutes at 265 to 285°F (130 to 140°C) without steam.

▲ **8.** The black superimposed design now has volume, which strongly contrasts with the first impression and with the pattern on the fabric.

◄ **9.** The final printed fabric.

Repeated Patterns

Creating pieces with a repeated pattern means taking a motif and extending it across the fabric, repeating it according to a determined sequence. This requires creating a motif with the design (see page 56). After creating the motif, assuming that it repeats in all directions, it is important to establish the dimensions of the repeated motif based on the screen, that is, to register the screen on the fabric. Registering the screen serves as a guide for establishing the placement of each impression; in other words, it helps discover the best placement of the screen for extending the pattern on the entire piece of fabric according to the repeated motif. If the printing were to go ahead without registering the screen, it could create poor alignment between the different impressions, leaving irregular spaces between motifs, thus causing am imperfect print.

The register for the screen is based on the repeated motif; it includes the outside of the screen and creates a grid based on the repetition across and down the fabric according to the dimensions of the screen and the location of the motif with respect to the previous one. The result is a grid on the fabric that will serve as a template for the printing process. Here, we will explain in detail a method of registering any printing screen on a fabric and then printing the motif. In this case, we will use the same screen used to print the background in the previous section (which conveniently has already been turned into a motif) to print white lacquer on a gray twill cotton and synthetic fabric.

▲ **1.** After the fabric is situated on the printing table and fixed with the tack spray adhesive, the original design module, or motif, is put in place. It must be straight and carefully aligned with respect to the sides of the fabric, and then it is fixed in place with the adhesive.

▲ **2.** The screen is very carefully placed over the original so that the design coincides exactly with the original; in other words, the white shapes on the screen are lined up with the black shapes on the original.

▶ **3.** The screen is held firmly in place, and a vanishing marker is used to mark its outline.

▲ **4.** The screen is lifted carefully, making sure the original stays in place, and it is moved over, aligning the previous vertical mark with the side of the frame and placing the design on the screen in the desired position with respect to the original module.

◀ **5.** The screen is placed in such a way that the shapes on it fit together and match those of the motif based on the original design. The empty spaces between the shapes in the design should correspond to the spaces between the different shapes of the original. If the proportions are not respected, the print will not have a continuous pattern when it is finished.

▼ **6.** With the screen in this position, the outside edge of the frame is marked on the fabric. The mark of the short side will be an extension of the first mark of the frame, while the upper part, or long side (marked in the photograph) will create a new transversal line.

▼ **7.** Without moving the screen, the extension or location of the centerline of the outline of the first screen is marked on the frame. Hold a straightedge or a stick above the line marked in the fabric that can be seen through the transparent screen, and mark each side and the tops of the frame strips. This mark will help to line up the screen during the printing process.

▲ **8.** The process is repeated on the other side of the original design. The screen is placed so that the long side is an extension of the transverse line of the first screen, and with the shapes of the design correctly aligned to each other, the outline of the frame is marked with the vanishing marker.

▲ **9.** Using the stick, mark the position of the vertical line marked on the fabric (short side) of the first screen on the frame.

▼ **10.** Move the screen toward the side until the line on the frame corresponds to the vertical mark on the fabric, and the line of the two short sides coincide with the horizontal line of the screen on the fabric. Then trace the outline with the marker.

▼ **11.** Continue this work in both directions, forward and to the side, moving the screen following the previous steps and tracing the perimeter with the marker. The result is a grid that will serve as a reference for the print.

▲ **12.** To begin the printing process the screen is placed on the first mark, aligning the sides of the frame with the lines on the fabric (the first perimeter outlined). The impression is created with a single pass and is then allowed to dry.

▲ **13.** The screen is moved to the side, aligning the sides with the lines on the fabric and the lines on the frame strips with the vertical and horizontal lines with the marked centerlines. It is printed and allowed to dry. Then we move forward, placing the frame in the same way, with the sides of the frame on the lines of the fabric and the marks on the frame aligned with the corresponding vertical and horizontal lines. Always strive to avoid making errors.

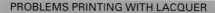

PROBLEMS PRINTING WITH LACQUER

Defective Ink

The result of printing too fast, with too little pressure, or with ink that is starting to dry, can be an impression that is not very opaque and allows the color of the fabric to show through.

Excess Ink

A pass with a squeegee loaded with too much ink or two passes can cause the lacquer to accumulate on the fabric and cause unsightly buildup.

► **14.** Here is the fabric after the printing is finished.

Devoré and Bleaching

Devoré and bleaching are two printing methods that are based on using techniques that, unlike block printing and serigraphy, are not based on the creation of a printed color.

Although they can make use of serigraphy techniques and have some aspects in common, they also have their own very specific methods and processes that make them their own medium. Both techniques are based on modifying some qualities of the fabric to which they are applied. So, rather than modifying the look of the fabric by adding colors of volumes (like relief ink), they vary the nature of the fabric. Devoré affects the texture of the fabric, creating areas where one part of it is eliminated by chemical action, to leave the base fabric exposed. Bleaching affects the color, creating—again through chemical action—areas with colors that are different from the original fabric.

Devoré

Devoré is a technical process that consists of making an impression with a caustic chemical, which, after drying and in the presence of heat, destroys specific kinds of fibers in the fabric and leaves others intact. There are different chemicals for devoré; some destroy protein fibers and others destroy cellulose fibers. They are available from different manufacturers as either gels or preparations for mixing in the studio. However, commercial two-component gels (manufactured by DuPont) make the work easier, because they are quick and easy to prepare and allow you to mix a desired quantity at the moment you are going to use it. This product is mainly used with velvet fabrics that are composed of viscose in the nap and silk in the base fabric, or satin fabrics also composed of silk and viscose. The devoré destroys cellulose fibers like cotton and linen, as well as regenerated fibers created from cellulose, like rayon and viscose.

▲ Dolors Noguer, *Petjades de Barcelona,* 2006. A series of scarves inspired by the forms of the pavement tiles in the city of Barcelona. Etched silk and viscose velvet, with later added silk gauze lining and colored with selective dye. 53.5 × 9 inches (136 × 23 cm) each.

▶ **1.** An original design by Elisa Rubió, drawn in ink on tracing paper, will be applied to silk and viscose velvet using the devoré technique. When preparing the original design it is very important to decide beforehand which parts you want to be etched—which means with the base fabric visible—and which parts of the velvet will stay the same. The black areas of the original will stay open on the printing screen (see "Exposure," page 79); these are the areas that will be burned out, while the transparent areas will remain obstructed and the velvet will remain unscathed. In this image you can see two versions of the same design with two approaches to the devoré. In the design on the left, the devoré will configure the motif; in the design synthetic fibers on the right the devoré will create the outlines and details of the motif.

On the other hand, it does not affect synthetic fibers or the protein-based fibers like silk. The results will vary according to the composition and structure of the fabric, so it is a good idea to run some tests on pieces of fabric similar to the one you will use before beginning the process. Although it can be applied with a brush, the best results are attained with serigraphy, because the pressure you apply ensures that the chemical will penetrate the fabric and completely permeate it.

Devoré does not require an especially complex process. The chemical is always applied to the back of the fabric; after it is dry it is activated by applying controlled heat until the fibers turn brown; finally, it is rinsed with a large amount of water. After the chemical is applied to the fabric the process is completed as soon as possible, because if the product stays on very long it can affect all the fibers. In the following example demonstrated by Joan Albert Sánchez using an original design by Elisa Rubió, you will see the working method for etching a velvet fabric. The technique is also similar for satin fabrics.

▼ It is possible to achieve very detailed forms with the devoré technique, as you can see in these samples of silk and viscose velvet that were etched and then dyed.

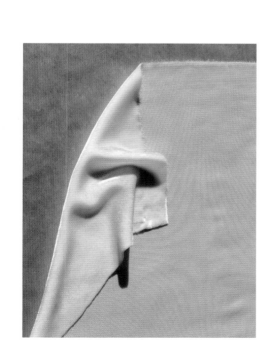

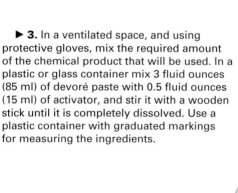

▲ **2.** We have chosen to use the version where the devoré will establish the outlines of the image. The motif is transferred to the printing screen (see page 75). Notice that the black areas of the design are the ones that remain open in the mesh of the screen, without the pink emulsion.

▶ **3.** In a ventilated space, and using protective gloves, mix the required amount of the chemical product that will be used. In a plastic or glass container mix 3 fluid ounces (85 ml) of devoré paste with 0.5 fluid ounces (15 ml) of activator, and stir it with a wooden stick until it is completely dissolved. Use a plastic container with graduated markings for measuring the ingredients.

▶ **4.** Place the velvet on the printing table, which has been covered with kraft paper, with the backside facing up.

▲ **5.** The screen is put in the desired position, with the bottom in contact with the fabric. Pour the product with utmost care along one edge of the screen, between the frame and the image, on the blocked part of the mesh.

▲ **6.** Hold the screen firmly with one hand and use your other hand to spread the paste with a squeegee. Apply pressure while holding the squeegee at a 45-degree angle, making several passes in both directions to make sure that the product penetrates the fabric.

◄ **7.** The screen should then be carefully lifted on one of its long sides so the fabric will pull away, avoiding contact with the skin. Wash the screen with a lot of water and set the fabric aside to dry.

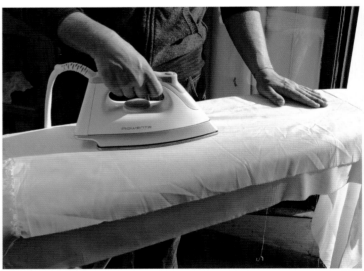

▲ **8.** The devoré paste is activated by applying heat. To do so, place the fabric between two clean white cloths and set it on an ironing board with the backside facing up. In a well-ventilated room, iron the fabric with a household iron set to medium temperature and with the steam turned off.

◄ **9.** The fibers of the velvet, which were originally white, turn brown. Keeping an eye on the pattern, continue ironing until the brown tone is uniform, regulating the temperature of the iron if necessary. If you iron for too long or apply too much heat, the fibers will turn blackish and the project will be ruined; conversely, if they stay white it will be necessary to apply more heat.

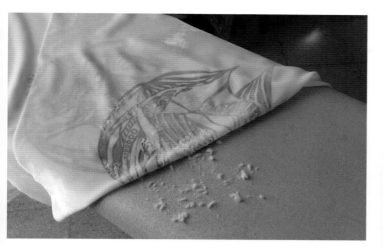

◄ **10.** In this phase of the project the viscose fibers will begin coming off the fabric.

▼ **11.** Wash the velvet, lightly scrubbing it under running water. The viscose fibers of the velvet will come off the fabric easily and stay in the water.

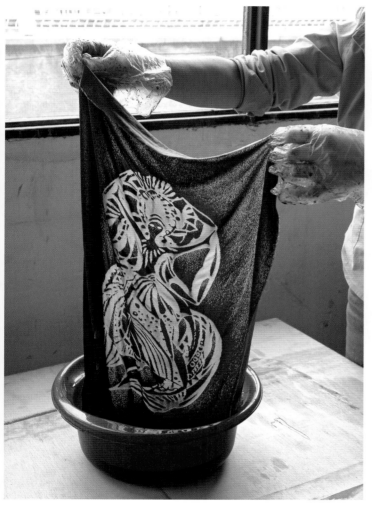

▲ **12.** You can create interesting effects by dying velvet that has been etched. In this case, we chose to use a reactive dye that was applied cold.

► **13.** Here is the velvet, etched with devoré paste and then dyed. The difference between the colors of the viscose nap and the silk base fabric emphasizes the advantages of the devoré process.

Bleaching

Bleaching is a technique that is used to change the original color of the fabric by removing color from its fibers; in some cases the fabric may turn almost white. This is an easy and inexpensive process, since the bleaching agent can be prepared in the studio. It can be applied with a brush or a printing screen, and the best results are obtained on dyed cotton fabrics such as denim. With other fabrics, especially synthetics, bleaching can produce very different tonal variations from the original color of the fabric; therefore, it is a good idea to experiment with the product on scrap pieces of the same material before using it on the final project. It is important to remember that different concentrations of the bleaching agent (sodium hypochlorite, or bleach) in the mixture will produce different bleached colors. The three most common concentrations are: 25 percent bleach with 75 percent water for a soft bleached effect, 50 percent bleach and 50 percent water for a medium bleached effect, and 75 percent bleach to 25 percent water for a complete bleached effect. It is important to use pure bleach, that is, no detergents or scents added, and to purchase bleach from a reputable manufacturer, because there are some sodium hypochlorite solutions that produce less than desirable results.

In this example, developed by Joan Albert Sánchez, we will demonstrate the bleaching process. We will use the screen print technique on synthetic satin fabric, which produces very different colors from cotton fabrics, as we will see later in the "Step-by-Step" section. We will also show how to create a screen by applying reserves directly to it, without using photo emulsion. The reserves are construction paper cutouts, stickers, and acrylic paint, although paper, plastic contact paper, white glue or wax, and other items can be used as well. However, these materials may not withstand the pressure exerted on screen prints; therefore, it may only last a few prints.

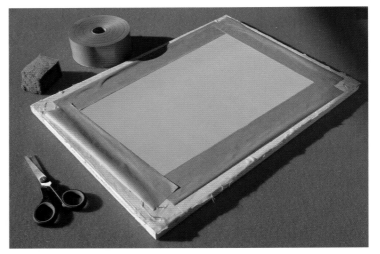

◄ **1.** The reserves are applied directly to the screen. We placed masking tape on the bottom, along the joints between the screen and the frame, to define the printing area. Since we wanted to create an uneven effect, we glued the tape without paying too much attention to symmetry; then we let them dry.

▲ **2.** We cut out undulating strips of construction paper of different widths, long enough to cover the frame from side to side over the masking tape.

► **3.** The strips were glued onto the screen with universal glue made of cellulose nitrate (nitrocellulose); then we let them dry.

► **4.** Next, we added the round stickers and painted other circular motifs with acrylic paint; then they were left to dry.

▼ **5.** Here are the finished reserves on the screen. The negative impression of these motifs will be the bleached areas, that is, the areas that are uncovered on the screen, while the fabric will have the original color in the areas that were under the reserved motifs.

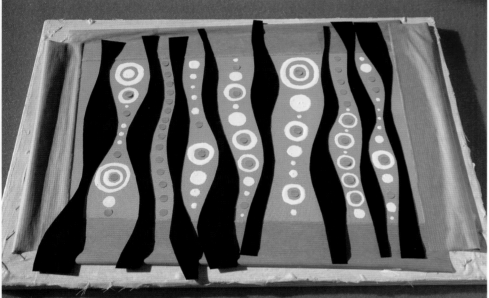

▼ **6.** The bleaching paste was prepared by mixing methylcellulose glue, water, and bleach (sodium hypochlorite) in a plastic or glass container, not metal.

◄ **7.** We poured some bleach inside the plastic or glass container and added the same amount of water to make a 1:1 mixture, equal parts of bleach and water. Then, we added the methylcellulose glue slowly, stirring with a wooden or plastic spoon (but not metal) until the paste became fluid. The proportions of bleach will vary depending on the tone that we want to achieve, which will depend also on the type of fiber or fabric. Therefore, we recommend that you experiment beforehand on scraps of fabric with paste containing different concentrations of bleach.

► **8.** We chose to use a very dark greenish-blue synthetic satin fabric. We placed the fabric on the table that was covered with kraft paper, secured it with tack adhesive spray, and then placed the screen in contact with the fabric with the desired alignment.

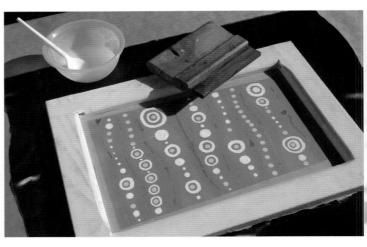

▼ **9.** We placed a line of bleaching paste inside the frame, along one of the narrow sides.

► **10.** While holding the frame firmly in place with one hand, we spread the paste with the other, spreading it with a continuous movement of the squeegee held at a 45-degree angle, first on one side of the screen.

▲ **11.** We finished spreading it on the rest of the screen, going over it several times to make sure that the impression was evenly covered and that the paste penetrated the fabric thoroughly. With the bleaching technique, unlike other printing techniques, it is not necessary to make the print on a single pass, because it is important for the fabric to be evenly covered with bleaching paste.

► **12.** The screen was removed very carefully by raising one side, and we lifted it without disturbing the fabric to avoid staining it by accident. Bleach is a potent agent, and any splashing or any contact of the fabric with the paste can cause staining.

◀ **13.** We hung the fabric in the sun to help it dry faster. Be very careful because the paste that is still wet can smear or drip, causing some areas to bleach accidentally.

▲ **14.** When the paste is dry, the bleached parts of the fabric will be stiff. To remove the paste (basically the dry methylcellulose glue) and arrest the effect of the bleach, wash it with running water.

◀ **15.** We finished neutralizing the effect of the bleach by submerging the fabric in a tub, preferably plastic, with a solution of 6 fluid ounces (200 ml) of vinegar per 1 quart (1 L) of water, and we let it soak for ten minutes. We removed it and hung it to dry. It is better not to wring it out too much.

▼ **16.** View of two pieces of bleached fabric created with different bleach concentrations. The fabric on the right has a deeper bleached effect resulting in more of a silvery tone, while the one on the left presents more of a yellow tone.

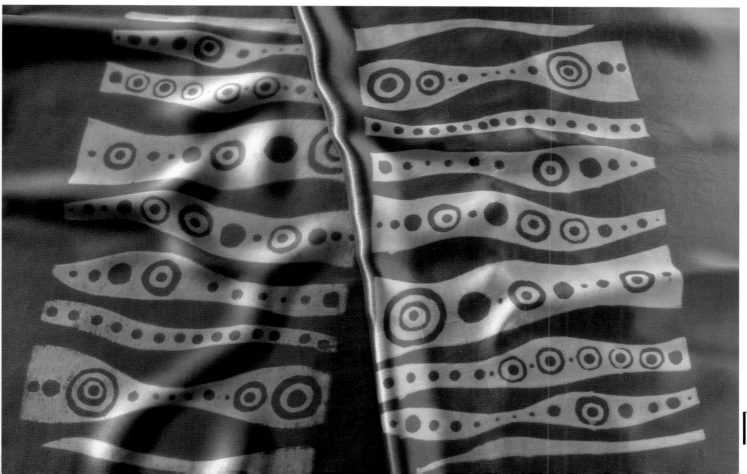

RESERVE TECHNIQUES

In printing, reserve techniques are used to block out certain areas of the fabric in different ways, to prevent the dyes or the paint that will cover the rest of the fabric from affecting the reserved areas. Therefore, with these techniques the motifs are created with the reserves, which is the process that configures the design. The main reserve techniques are batik, where wax is used to create the reserves, which is followed by dyeing; serti, in which the reserves are mainly made with gutta (wax can also be used), and then paint is applied. There are other methods in which reserves can be created by making folds or knots, or by braiding, twisting, or pressing—all of which are classified under the category of Shibori. The knotting technique is also known as tie-dye, although none of these techniques will be covered here because they go beyond the scope of this book.

Batik

Batik is a word that originated in Java and probably comes from the word *ambatik,* meaning "to write and draw." In Indonesia, the suffix *-tik* means "dot," "small drop," or "to make dots," in other words, to make clothes with small dots. It could also come from the word *tritik,* which is the name given to a printing technique done with reserves created by knotting and sewing, after which the fabric is dyed. It is considered a very old technique and is used especially in India, Southeast and Central Asia, and Africa, although pieces of Indian fabric made with batik have been found in Egyptian tombs dating back to the first century A.D., and some pre-Colombian fabrics have also been made with this printing technique.

Generally, batik is applied to cotton fabrics, but it can also be used on silk and other natural fibers. The technique consists of creating reserves on the fabric by applying melted wax, which is followed by dyeing once the wax has cooled off. The wax can be applied with tjanting tools, art or all-purpose brushes, and with printing blocks. The latter system was created in Java in the mid-nineteenth century as a way to meet the growing demand with cheap, easy, and quick manufacturing processes. The reserve blocks out the fabric and preserves its original color throughout the dyeing process. Generally, there are several reserve steps with subsequent dyeing phases, which give way to the print. The background color will result from the various dyeing steps and will be the sum of all the colors, which are combined according to the subtractive mixture of the color (see page 60). Therefore, it will be necessary to plan all the dyeing phases, beginning with the lighter colors up to the darkest. In a process involving different dyes, the areas covered with wax will remain the color of the fabric that was beneath. So, the first wax reserve will protect the fabric; the second, the first dye; the third, the second dye, and so on. Although it is not difficult, it is important to understand the method, because this is an interesting medium for experimenting with color and form.

One of the characteristics of batik is the cracking effect, which results from the dye penetrating the cracks (formed in the wax) that occur while handling the fabric during the dyeing process. Depending on the type of wax used and its manipulation, a lesser or greater cracking effect can be produced. This enhances the work and quality of the final product.

▶ Elisa Rubió, 2007. Central piece for a bed cover. Batik and direct paint over cotton taffeta, 98.5 × 35.5 inches (250 × 90 cm).

The wax for the batik reserves can be store-bought and ready for use, which simplifies the process; however, it can also be prepared in the studio. Making your own wax is always cheaper and helps to control all the phases of the process, because it will fit exactly the requirements of your project. Therefore, you can prepare different types of waxes made with different compositions based on your particular needs. To make the wax for batik, mix beeswax with paraffin in a container and heat it up until the liquid is melted evenly. Generally, it is mixed in a 50/50 proportion, in other words, equal amounts of wax and paraffin. However, if you want to achieve a deep batik cracking effect, mix 70 percent paraffin and 30 percent wax. Of course, these proportions can be changed according to your specific needs; keep in mind, though, that the greater the proportion of paraffin the greater the cracking results. The preparation is fast and easy; you can even prepare an additional amount and store it for future use.

▶ **2.** If you wish to store wax for future use, let it cool off first, after you strain it to remove any impurities. You can use a regular kitchen strainer with a piece of nylon fabric.

◀ **1.** To prepare the wax for the batik that we will show in the following pages, we mixed equal parts of beeswax and paraffin in a fire-proof container, and we heated on medium temperature until the liquid was evenly melted.

◀ **3.** Place a wood frame on a waterproof surface; in this case, we used a table covered with melamine. Secure the frame firmly to prevent the wax from seeping out, and pour the hot wax slowly inside the frame while it is being strained.

▲ **4.** Let the wax cool down to room temperature. Then, cut it into small chunks, which will make it easier to store and preserve. With a kitchen knife, cut thin vertical strips on the wax, followed by horizontal ones. You will end up with small squares, which will be ready for use with any size tjanting, no matter how small.

▲ **5.** Remove the frame carefully and scrape the wax from the melamine surface with a spatula or a scraper.

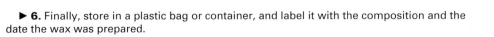

▶ **6.** Finally, store in a plastic bag or container, and label it with the composition and the date the wax was prepared.

Making the Batik

The idea behind the batik technique is to block areas of the fabric with reserves to repel the color when the fabric is submerged in the dye. Therefore, the fabric's design is defined by the motifs created with the wax. When using this technique it is important to plan the wax reserves and the subsequent dyeing steps carefully. The dyeing solution should be cold or at the lowest temperature possible to avoid problems with the reserves; otherwise the wax could soften and come off, rendering the reserve unusable. Below, in a demonstration by Joan Albert Sánchez, we explain the process for creating any type of batik in a three-step dyeing process, as well as how to create cracking effects. For our project, we used cotton taffeta and cold reactive dyes. We drew the reserves freehand, although a prepared design can be used to print directly by placing it under the fabric, if it is transparent enough, or by transferring it to the fabric with a disappearing ink pen.

◄ **1.** Before we began we washed the fabric to eliminate the stiffness, and we ironed it. Then, the stretcher frame was assembled (made of wood, adjustable, and set to the desired size) and covered it with a piece of fabric larger than the frame.

► **2.** The piece was mounted onto the frame with pushpins. First, we pinned down one of the corners; then, after stretching the fabric perfectly, the other three corners were attached.

◄ **3.** Next, a pushpin was added in the center on each side of the frame, making sure that the fabric was stretched out at all times. Finally, the remaining pushpins were added in all the sides at regular intervals. The tautness of the fabric is an important aspect of this technique, because if it touches the work surface during the process, the wax could stick to it; this would cause smearing and the design would be ruined.

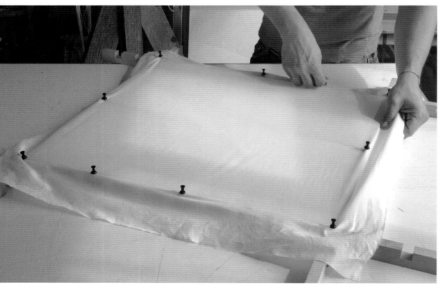

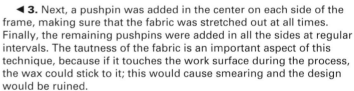

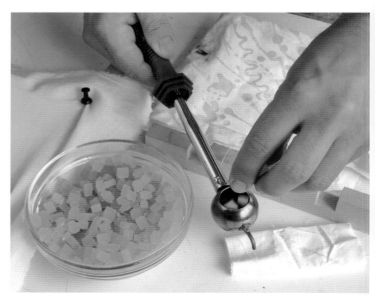

► **4.** To make the first reserve, we used an electric tjanting. We inserted a few pieces of wax in the bowl and we turned it on. We placed it over a fabric scrap until the wax began to flow; more wax pieces can be added if needed. To transfer the bowl to the fabric we covered the tip with a piece of fabric to prevent it from dripping.

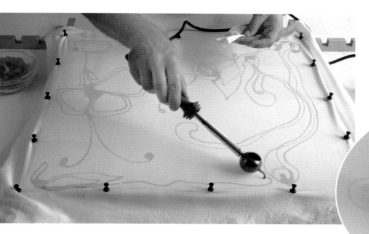

◄ **5.** We began drawing on the fabric at a quick pace. The electric tjanting heats up the wax continuously, which comes out of a tip that is quite wide. In this phase, the wax will reserve the original color of the fabric; in other words, the covered areas will remain white.

◄ **6.** When we needed to lift the bowl from the fabric, we covered the tip with the scrap of fabric, again to stop the flow and avoid staining the fabric. Finally, we turned off the tjanting and let the reserves dry.

◄ **7.** We prepared the dye in a plastic tub, wide enough to dip in the fabric, following the manufacturer's instructions on the package. We poured enough cold water to cover the batik, a can of turquoise dye dissolved in a small amount of hot water, an envelope of fixative also dissolved the same way, and 4.5 ounces (125 g) of salt. We then let it cool down.

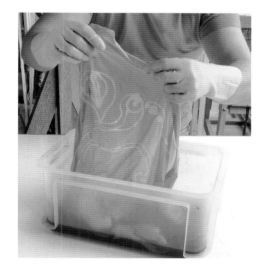

► **8.** We removed the pins and the fabric from the frame and submerged it carefully in the dye. (Always use gloves to protect your hands.)

We submerged the fabric little by little, stirring it gently and continuously to make sure that the dye spread evenly. Generally, we recommend a dyeing time of sixty minutes, although the fabric can be removed before if you want a lighter shade. When the color dries it will look lighter than the dye.

◄ 9. We hung the piece to air dry. In this first phase the reserve is white while the rest of the fabric is turquoise. We kept this reserve until the end of the process.

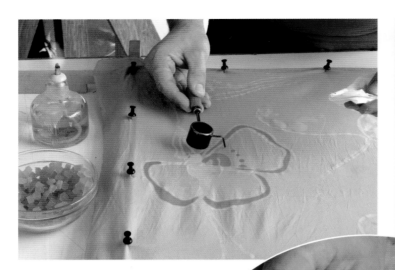

▲ **10.** When the fabric was dry, we set it back on the stretcher frame, making sure that the pushpin holes were aligned and the fabric was taut. Then, we made the turquoise reserves. This time we used a regular tjanting with a thinner tip.

▲ **11.** We inserted a few pieces of wax and heated it up over the flame. To prevent it from dripping we covered the tip with a scrap of fabric.

◄ **12.** We drew the lines that we wanted to remain turquoise.

► **13.** In this photograph we can see both reserves: the first one in white, and the second one covering the turquoise background, looking a little bit lighter than the fabric due to the effect of the reserves.

◄ **14.** We prepared an olive-green solution and dyed the fabric following the process explained before. The color of the areas that were not reserved will have a green shade resulting from adding turquoise to the olive-green.

► **15.** We placed the fabric back on the stretcher and made the reserves that will have the new green color. This time we used the electric tjanting to draw them.

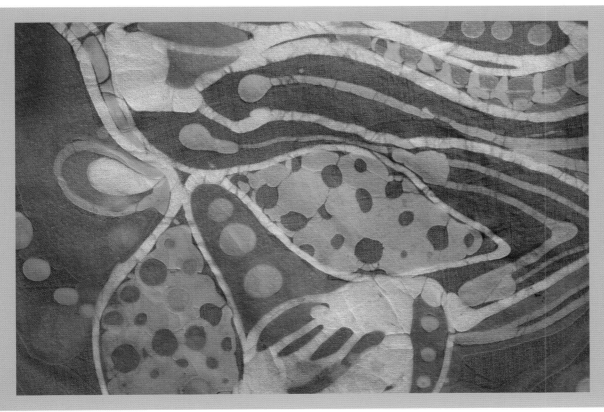

◄ **16.** In this picture we can see the three reserve phases: the first one in white, the second turquoise, and the third one in green, which looks somewhat darker because of the wax.

◄ **17.** We prepared the purple solution and dyed the fabric according to the process already explained. Notice how the dye adheres to the areas that are not covered with wax. The background color is a combination of the three dyes: turquoise, olive-green, and purple.

► **18.** In this last step we cracked the wax to create a dark cracked effect. We squeezed the fabric with both hands several times, changing the position to cause the wax to crack in different directions.

▼ **19.** In this picture we can see the dye phases with reserves: the first one in white, the second in turquoise, the third one in green, and the last one of the dark background. We can also see the characteristic cracked look of batik.

▲ **20.** A view of the batik finished and dry. At this point the wax was still on the fabric, so we needed to remove it.

◄ **21.** We placed the batik between two sheets of blotting paper, with a piece of thicker fabric on the bottom and another one on top.

▲ **22.** We then applied heat with an iron set on high without the steam. We went over the same area several times.

▲ **23.** The blotting paper absorbs the wax, which sticks to it. We repeated the process with a clean sheet of blotting paper until all the wax was removed.

▼ **24.** The batik is finished and wax-free.

Serti

Serti is a French word that means "to inlay," and by association the term is used to define the screen-printing technique, which prints reserves—mainly with gutta—to block out the areas from the dye. Therefore, serti is the technique used to reserve the areas that surround those that need to be dyed, defining their borders as well as their forms. The areas of color appear as if they were inlaid inside a frame.

Generally, serti is considered one of the more recent printing techniques, although its origin is not very clear. Some authors claim that its origins are rooted in the traditions of Indonesia, where the tree from which gutta is extracted originated. However, there is no proof of this. Whatever the origin may be, it appears that this technique spread during the twentieth century from Eastern Europe. Strictly speaking, serti is a technique that forms part of the wider field of silk painting, which involves other techniques as well, such as direct painting or creating effects using gradations, salt, thickeners, or alcohol, which will not be covered here because they fall outside the scope of this book.

Next, in an exercise designed by Joan Albert Sánchez, we will show the versatility of this technique. We will explain the basics of serti and the two methods of creating reserves, as well as how to use gutta directly, with specific comments on the painting process. It should not be taken as a comprehensive explanation of painting, which would go beyond the scope of this book. We are using the techniques that provide the most expressive results from an artistic point of view, which can be adapted to create personal and innovative designs.

This technique does not require any more ability than other techniques presented in this book; however, we recommend that those who are not familiar with the subject do some testing on scraps of fabric before tackling a project.

Working with Serti

Serti is created by printing the outline of the design with gutta, which can be applied directly from the tube or with an applicator. The outline will define the reserve, which will remain in place when the process is finished. If the gutta is colorless, the outline will be of the underlying color of the fabric, and if the gutta has a particular color, the outline will be that color. Once the reserves have been made, the gutta is left to dry and the paint is applied. The paint will be contained inside each reserve, within the defined borders and with the desired shape, and will not run onto the rest of the fabric. However, gutta has other applications that go beyond making borders. It can be used to make designs directly on the fabric as if it were a drawing or a painting (see following pages). Serti is not limited to gutta alone for making reserves, but it can also use wax to block out areas of work.

▼ María Roca, 2006. Scarf (detail), mixed technique on gauze silk. 98.5 × 19.625 inches (250 × 50 cm).

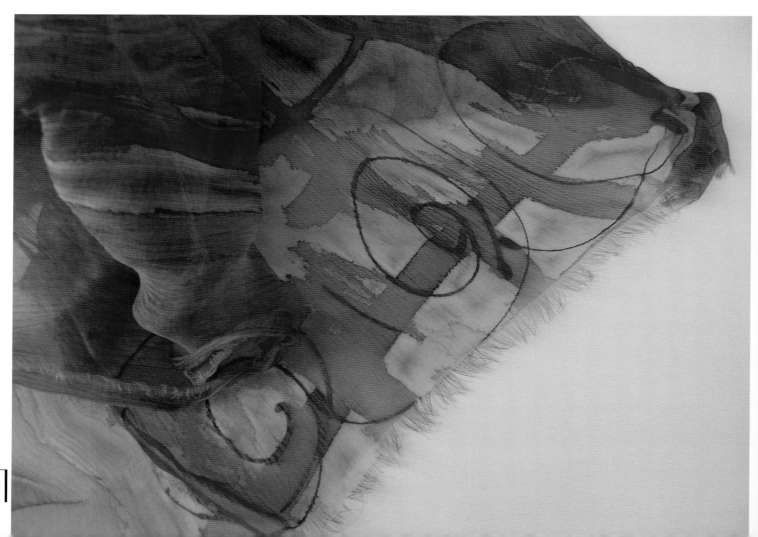

P rint designs are defined with reserves made by applying gutta directly onto the fabric, which, once finished, must be left to dry completely. To make sure that the gutta application is correct, that is, that there are no thin or broken-up lines, it is inspected by holding it against the light. If needed, the forms are reinforced with another application of gutta. This point is important, because to make a strong enough border for the paint, the gutta must permeate the fabric completely. Otherwise, the paint would bleed through to the fabric beyond the confined area of the print and would ruin the work.

Next, we will show how to create prints using gutta reserves on a gauze silk scarf. We use water-based colorless gutta, which will create reserves of the color of the fabric, and alcohol-based paints that are steam-fixed. First, we apply a background color wash to the fabric; then, once the reserves have been made, we apply the color mixed on wet as well. The colors will blend together, as with any other printing technique, depending on the subtractive color mixture (see page 60). It is also possible to use gutta as paint, drawing over the painted surfaces or making lines that will be reserved once the paint is applied.

◀ **1.** Before the work begins, it is a good idea to wash the fabric to eliminate the stiffness, and to iron it. This gauze is worked on directly. First, we assembled the stretcher frame, which in this case is made of wood and is movable, adjusting it to the size of the scarf because it is larger than the latter. Since it did not have any supports, we used wood blocks to make legs, which were attached to the frame with masking tape to elevate the frame. By doing this we prevented the fabric from touching the work surface in case it sagged when wetted, since this could cause staining.

◀ **2.** We placed the scarf within the stretcher, attaching it with fabric suspension hooks. First, we attached one of the corners with a hook on each side of it. We used strings of knit fabric to connect them to the frame because they are good to hold the fabric in place and can be adjusted by loosening or tightening according to the desired tension. The suspension hooks were attached at the very edge of the scarf.

▶ **3.** The other corners were attached, adjusting the hooks until the fabric was perfectly taut.

▶ **4.** Then, we continued with the sides, attaching one hook at the center of each side.

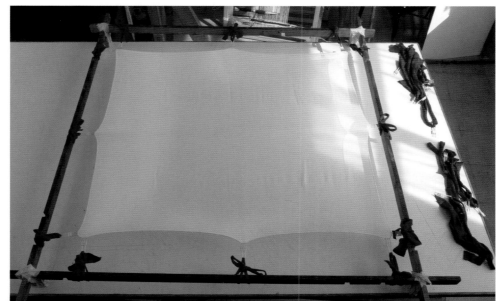

◀ **5.** Finally, we placed two hooks at regular intervals on each side.

▶ **6.** In this exercise we wanted the scarf to have a color background; since we used colorless gutta, the reserves will have the original white color of the silk and will contrast too much with the print. To achieve an even color background we worked on wet, which allows the paint to flow better. We applied thinner with a wide, all-purpose bristle brush.

◀ **7.** Then, with the same brush, we applied the back-ground color, which in this case was green mixed with equal parts of thinner; we then let it dry.

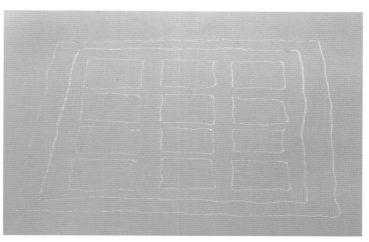

▲ **8.** We drew the reserves for the scarf's central motif with water-based colorless gutta, applied directly from the tube fitted with a tip.

▲ **9.** When the reserves were finished, we made sure that the gutta was sturdy enough, letting it dry afterwards. The drying time depends on the type and brand of gutta, and the environment in the shop. If needed, you can use a hair dryer set on cool to speed up the drying time.

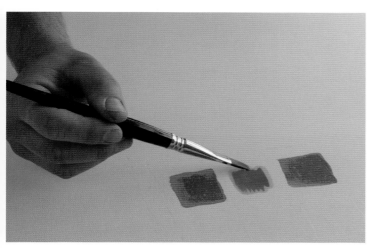

▲ **10.** First, we painted the design's lower squares. The paint was applied inside each area with a medium flat, soft squirrel-hair brush. It was not necessary to slide the brushes all the way to the edge of the area, because the paint spread until it touched the gutta, which held it in place.

▲ **11.** Then, we applied the background paint, followed by the outer border, blocked out by the reserve of the motif's perimeter; we then let it dry.

◄ **12.** The design finished. The colors look well-defined inside the squares bordered by the gutta lines, which are the color of the fabric.

Reserves with Wax

Wax reserves are used for the same purpose as gutta reserves: to define the outlines of the areas that are to be painted. After preparing the wax (see page 97) it can be applied to the fabric with an art brush, an all-purpose brush, or a tjanting. Then, it is left to cool, after which the paint can be applied. It can be removed by applying heat, as it was described for batik (see page 103). The reserves will have the underlying color of the fabric, which will provide contrast against the painted areas. In the following pages, we will explain how to make wax reserves using an all-purpose brush. Different brushes can produce different effects on the fabric because of their marks and the playful designs created by the paint running into the crevices between the reserves. Both types of reserves can be combined; gutta can be used after wax.

◀ **1.** When the central motif was completely dry, we proceeded with the wax reserves. We melted the wax on a hot plate and applied it to the fabric with a medium, all-purpose bristle brush, creating a grid of intersecting lines of different widths.

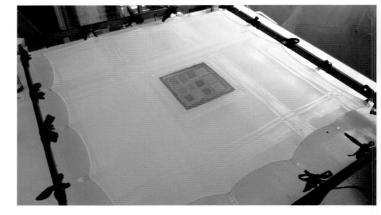

▶ **2.** The finished reserves. Some lines are more irregular than others. We let the wax cool off.

▼ **3.** Gutta can also be used over wax to create lines over the previous reserves. In this case, a few designs were drawn with the translucent gutta and left to dry.

▲ **4.** Then, we painted every area of the scarf outlined with reserves with a soft, wide, flat brush. Some colors were the result of mixing several colors in a container, while others were applied directly. Whenever we wanted to mix colors directly on the fabric, we worked on wet; in other words, we applied the paint while the previous one was still wet.

◀ **5.** We painted the inside of the gutta reserves with a flat, medium soft-hair brush.

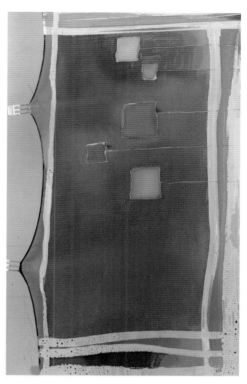

▲ 6. We continued painting with a soft-hair, all-purpose brush. We also painted over the reserves and in the crevices left by the brush when the wax was applied.

▲ 7. The overlapping technique and mixing colors on wet produced interesting gradations and playful colors. Notice how the transparent lines of gutta contrast against the colors. The paint that was applied over the wax formed droplets, which in some areas left an imprint on the fabric.

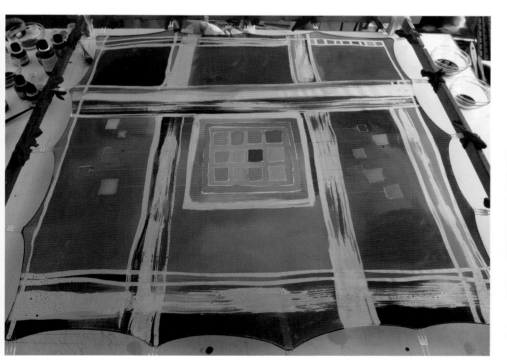

▲ 8. The painted scarf. We let it dry.

▶ 9. We removed the wax following the process explained for batik. Then, we removed the scarf from the frame and placed it under two sheets of blotting paper, with a thick fabric at the bottom and a similar one on top. Then, we applied heat with an iron set on high without the steam, going over the same area several times. We repeated the process after replacing the paper penetrated with wax with a clean one to avoid wax stains.

Painting with Color Gutta

Gutta is not only used for reserves; it is also used to print, make designs, and decorate motifs that had already been printed, or to paint on the fabric. Therefore, guttas of different colors and finishes (metallic, among others) provide a wide range of possibilities. For example, it can be used to create borders on articles of clothing and other items, which will replace hems because after it dries it prevents the fabric from fraying. Below, we will show how to create the details on the scarf with a black, gasoline-based gutta.

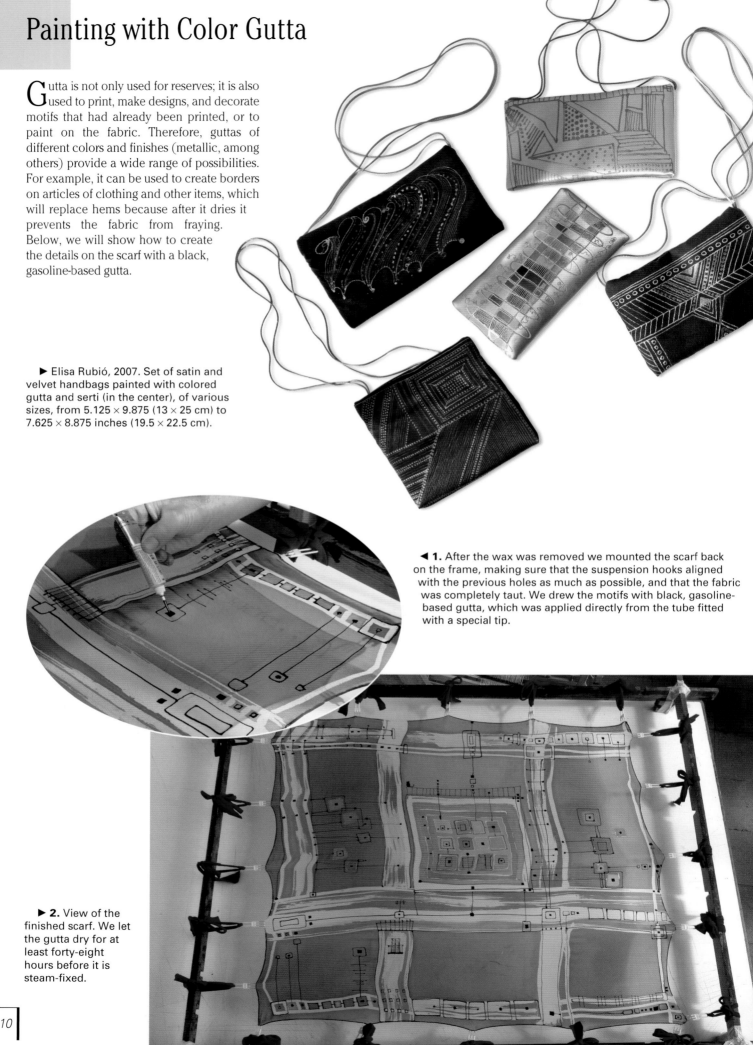

► Elisa Rubió, 2007. Set of satin and velvet handbags painted with colored gutta and serti (in the center), of various sizes, from 5.125 × 9.875 (13 × 25 cm) to 7.625 × 8.875 inches (19.5 × 22.5 cm).

◄ **1.** After the wax was removed we mounted the scarf back on the frame, making sure that the suspension hooks aligned with the previous holes as much as possible, and that the fabric was completely taut. We drew the motifs with black, gasoline-based gutta, which was applied directly from the tube fitted with a special tip.

► **2.** View of the finished scarf. We let the gutta dry for at least forty-eight hours before it is steam-fixed.

The final step of the serti technique is to fix the paint on the fabric. The alcohol-based paints, such as the ones we are using, are fixed with steam. Other paints are fixed by ironing them or by applying a specific product after they dry; some even become fixed as soon as they dry. Steam fixes the colors on the fabric permanently and enhances them at the same time, making them look brilliant and bright when the process is finished. The fabric becomes soft to the touch again, and it recovers its texture and original drape. Next, we will show how to fix with a vertical steamer. To make the process more efficient, several pieces can be steamed at the same time, which saves time and money.

◄ **1.** After the scarf is taken off the stretcher frame, proceed with the steam setting. Place it over the kraft paper that is rolled around the cardboard tube in the steamer's mast. The cardboard tube acts as the support and should fit perfectly between the lower support and the upper cover of the mast. Then, roll the paper with the scarf. We recommend natural-color kraft paper (that is, unbleached paper), because the others do not have the same porosity, nor do they produce the desired results.

◄ **2.** To use all the resources more efficiently, you can fix several pieces at the same time, rolling them after the scarf and side-by-side if the format allows it. To prevent them from touching each other, leave a space between them and roll the tube one time around.

◄ **3.** After the pieces are rolled tightly, secure the paper with a piece of masking tape on one of its ends, so it stays in place on the cardboard tube. Remember that the bottom end will rest on the movable lower piece.

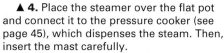

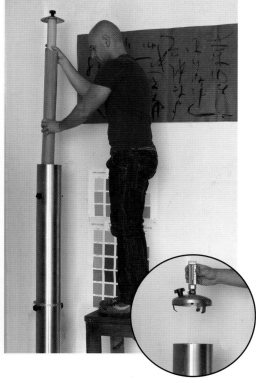

▲ **4.** Place the steamer over the flat pot and connect it to the pressure cooker (see page 45), which dispenses the steam. Then, insert the mast carefully.

Finally, cover it with the lid, which has a thermometer. It is steamed for three hours at a temperature above 212°F (100°C); in other words, once the inside temperature reaches 212°F (100°C), steam it for three hours. After this time, turn off and disconnect the pressure cooker, remove the lid, and let it cool.

► **5.** The finished scarf.

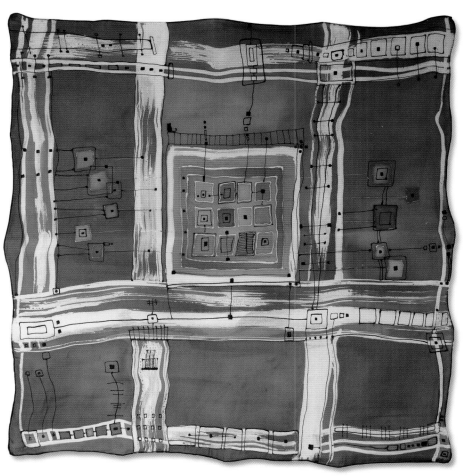

*I*n this final chapter we will present a series of step-by-step exercises in detail. There are six original projects in which the entire working process is explained, from the beginning to the finished piece. These exercises have been graded according to their level of difficulty, so you can move along in sequence from the first to the last. Some of the projects incorporate different techniques that are combined in the process of creating the piece, while others employ certain specific techniques but with a new approach, different from the normal application. All the exercises have been designed with you, the learner, in mind, combining various technical and formal resources. We hope that readers will find in them not only a model to copy, but also a source of inspiration and a guide for carrying out the work.

Step-by-
Step

Child's Dress

In this first step-by-step exercise you will be able to follow in full detail the process of block printing a toddler-sized orange dress made of cotton taffeta, designed by Elisa Rubió. In this exercise demonstrated by Miriam Albiñana, she will use a typical children's design as a decorative motif for the print, for which she has chosen a casual arrangement. To create the design, she has used various elements like blocks, used objects, recycled pieces, and office materials.

◄ **1.** This step-by-step exercise began with an existing dress onto which the artist has printed floral decorative motifs.

► **2.** To create the main flowers of the composition, the artist used a random object, a faucet handle to be more specific. The block was made by attaching the piece to a block of wood with contact glue.

► **3.** You can use an ironing board for this project because it provides the perfect support for the dress throughout the entire process. Place the dress, previously washed, on the ironing board. Insert a piece of cardboard in between, in this case lightweight cardboard, to avoid staining the surface and to provide a firm and hard support.

◄ 4. With a foam roller apply the blue color for the print on the block.

▼ 5. Print four flowers on the left half of the front of the dress. Make sure that the dress is always on top of the cardboard backing every time you print. Then, move the dress and print the next flower. Let them dry.

▼ 6. To print the stems, the artist used the edge of a wood block. The idea is not to have the stems go all the way to the bottom of the dress, but to stop just above the hem; therefore, that area can be protected with a newspaper. Next, print the stems with the edge of the block using blue printing paste.

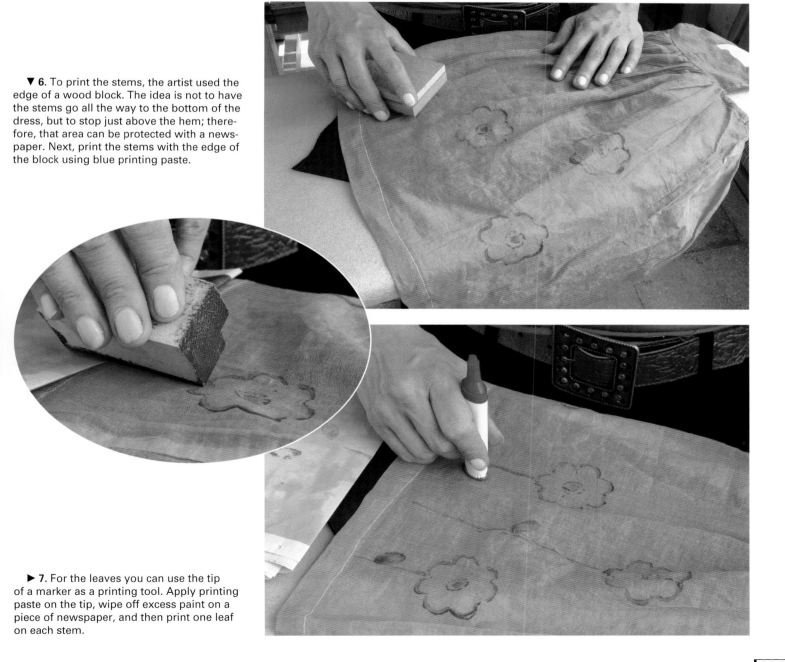

► 7. For the leaves you can use the tip of a marker as a printing tool. Apply printing paste on the tip, wipe off excess paint on a piece of newspaper, and then print one leaf on each stem.

◄ **8.** While the printed motifs are left to dry, begin making the blocks for the petals out of recycled bottle corks. Make two converging diagonals, beginning at a specific point and cutting carefully with a utility knife in such a way that the opposite side has approximately the shape of a quarter circle. Make two blocks.

► **9.** Use green, lemon-yellow, purple, and orange-yellow printing ink to print the petals as well.

◄ **10.** Place the paste on a plastic plate that you can use as a palette, and mix the colors until you get the combinations that you want.

► **12.** First, print the petals. To do this, dip the end of one of the cut corks in the color that you want.

◄ **11.** To print the petals, use the cork that you made, while the button in the center of the flowers can be painted with a regular cork that has not been cut. Use markers to print other leaves on the stems and secondary flowers.

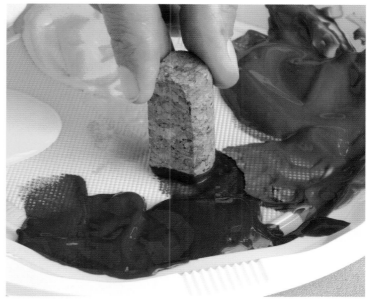

◄ **13.** Print the petals with different colors, aligning the rounded part of the base of the cork with the curvature of the flower. Alternate yellow, red, purple, and green for the different petals.

▼ **14.** Using the end of the cork that has not been cut out, paint the central button of the secondary flowers, one of them yellow and the other red. Print the petals with the end side of the marker, alternating similar colors as before.

► **15.** Before you continue, make sure that the printed motifs are completely dry. To speed up the drying process, you can use a hair dryer set on medium-high power and at low temperature.

◄ 16. Print the central buttons of the different blue flowers with the cork using purple, green, and red.

▲ 17. Finish the flowers by printing a few green leaves on their stems with a marker. If needed, the motifs already printed can be covered with a darker color. Here, the artist has covered a petal that was originally blue-green, using the same marker. Leave them to dry.

▲ 18. Print the secondary flowers (the ones with no stems) to create a combination of transparencies, which are achieved by overlapping new paint (that is, from mixing the first colors over the first prints that are already dry). Make each impression with a different color resulting from the mixture, that is, using the pastes to create a different color palette.

► 19. Use the marker to print a second set of petals.

► **20.** Decorate the neck of the dress with printed petals, using different shades of yellow, orange, purple, and red, and creating transparencies by overlapping. Once finished, leave the dress to dry and then iron it on the reverse side. Do not fold it when you store it, and do not wash it for at least fifteen days.

◄ **21.** This is how the finished dress looks.

Shawl with Gradated Colors

In this project we will explain how to print a wool taffeta shawl using two different techniques. The first phase will cover the printing of the three-color gradations; the second will explain how to print a motif on each end using silk screening. For both phases, silk and wool paints are used with specific processes that exemplify the multiple resources offered by them. They are used together with diluters and no-flow primer to complement what was explained in the chapter about serti (see page 104). Silk fabrics are normally used for gradations with shaded backgrounds; however, in this case, we will demonstrate the process on wool using a very similar technique to that used on silk. Project by Miriam Albiñana and Joan Albert Sánchez.

◄ **1.** Place the 63- by 13.75-inch (160- by 35-cm) wool shawl on a wood stretcher that is larger than the piece of fabric, and hold it in place with fabric hooks. The hooks are attached carefully to the hem and connected to the stretcher with thin strips of knit fabric, tightened until the shawl is stretched tautly. This will prevent the fabric from touching the surface of the worktable when it sags after it is dampened, which would cause the fabric to stain.

▼ **2.** The gradation results when the paints blend together in some areas of the fabric. Dampening the shawl with water helps the paint run.

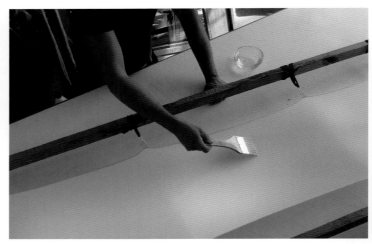

◄ **3.** To make the gradations, it is necessary to add a diluter to the paints. Here, the artist used a concentrated diluter, which previously had been mixed with distilled water. Following the recommendations provided by the manufacturer, mix 0.34 fluid ounces to 8.5 fluid ounces of water (10 ml to 250 ml); this is a proportion of 4:100.

► **4.** Gradation is a fast technique and results happen very quickly; that is why it is very important to prepare the correct amounts of paint needed and to gather all the brushes before you begin working. Pour the same amount of the prepared diluter in three dishes that are large enough to be able to dip all the brushes in them, even the wider ones. Next, pour the pink, orange, and green paint, which is fixed by steaming, in each one, adding more or less of them according to the level of saturation that you wish to obtain.

▲ **5.** Apply the paint beginning at each end and moving toward the center. Work quickly, and apply the paint with a wide, medium household brush using wide, side-to-side motions so the paint flows on the fabric.

▲ **6.** Several people working simultaneously at both ends will be needed to make large pieces; one will apply the pink paint while the other will apply the green. Each person will cover one-third of the fabric using a household brush and apply the paint quickly with wide, side-to-side brushstrokes.

◄ **7.** Orange will be applied on the central third of the fabric. To mix the colors by gradation, first add a small amount of paint with a small household brush in the areas that border the green and pink.

▼ **8.** Then, extend and spread the orange color with a household brush so it mixes with the other two colors. Go over the intersecting areas repeatedly so the colors blend together. If the gradation is applied to silk after each color application, blend the paint with a sponge around the areas where both colors meet.

◄ **9.** Continue applying the orange paint, moving toward the center of the piece. Work quickly and simultaneously.

▼ **10.** To finish, apply pure color in the center of the fabric, blending the brushstrokes together.

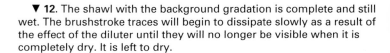

◄ **11.** Paint the fringes that adorn both ends of the shawl with their corresponding colors. Place a piece of paper, such as a newspaper, under the fringes, holding it with one hand and painting with the other, using a medium-hair household brush, until the color evens out with the rest of the fabric.

▼ **12.** The shawl with the background gradation is complete and still wet. The brushstroke traces will begin to dissipate slowly as a result of the effect of the diluter until they will no longer be visible when it is completely dry. It is left to dry.

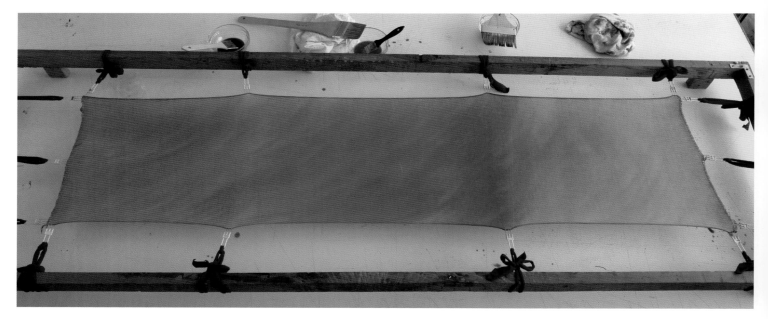

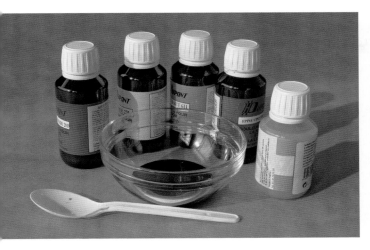

▲ **13.** For the silk screening use the same paint that was used before, mixed with a thickener. In this case, the artists wanted to create a deep chocolate color, so they mixed enough brown, gray, green, and pink paint in a large container until they obtained the color they wanted.

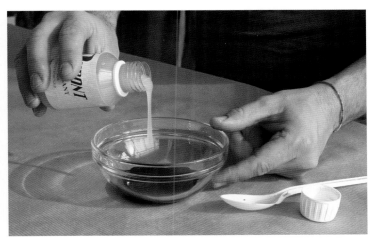

▲ **14.** Next, the thickener is added, which is mixed with the color in a 1:2 proportion, in other words, half as much thickener as paint. The thickener to screen-print on wool and silk can be replaced by methylcellulose glue, mixing it directly with the paint until the desired consistency is achieved.

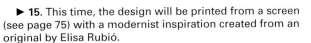

▶ **15.** This time, the design will be printed from a screen (see page 75) with a modernist inspiration created from an original by Elisa Rubió.

◀ **16.** The shawl is removed from the stretcher and placed perfectly flat on the printing table (which has been covered with kraft paper) with pins. The screen is lowered in alignment with the borders and according to the desired orientation of the motif, on one end of the shawl, until it comes in contact with the fabric. The floral motifs will be printed toward the inside of the piece, although given the nature of the design, it could also be printed with the floral elements facing outwards, that is, toward the side of the fringe.

◄ **17.** Place a line of paint on the right side of the screen with a plastic spoon, on the blocked-out area. Then, spread it with a squeegee at a 45-degree angle, applying pressure on it while dragging it smoothly over the motif. The width of the squeegee should cover the entire motif.

► **18.** Repeat the process to print the motif on the other side: place the screen opposite the previous printing, with the floral elements facing the inside of the piece.

◄ **19.** In both cases, the screen is lifted off the fabric very carefully by picking up on one of its corners. It is left to dry.

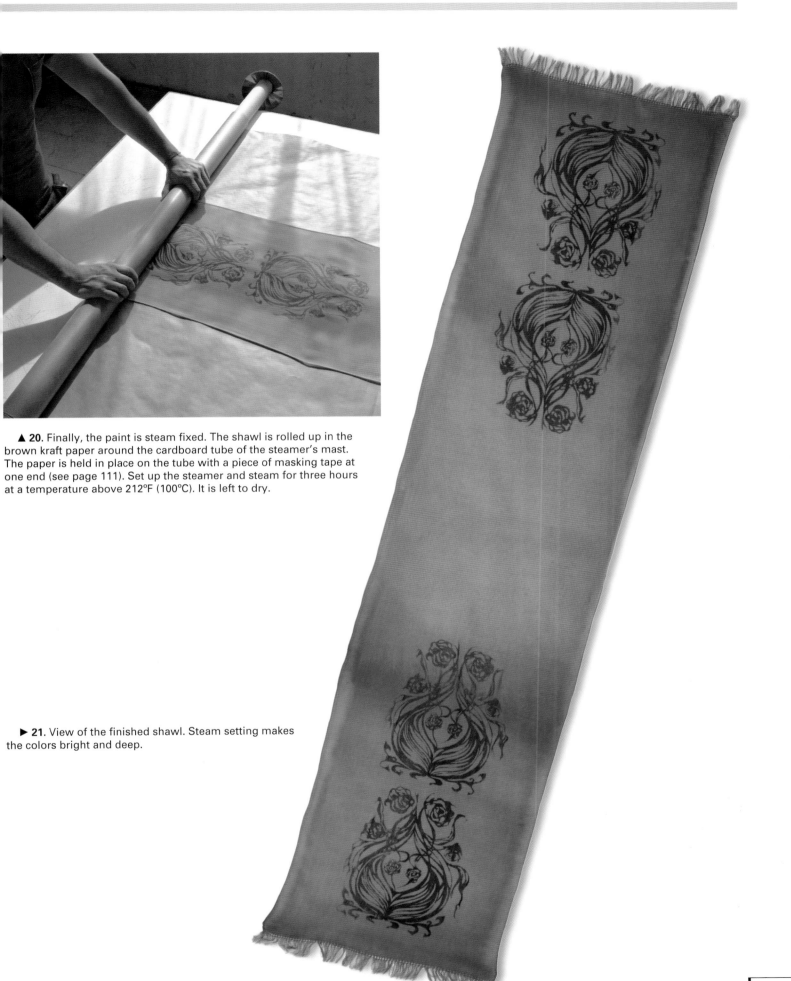

▲ **20.** Finally, the paint is steam fixed. The shawl is rolled up in the brown kraft paper around the cardboard tube of the steamer's mast. The paper is held in place on the tube with a piece of masking tape at one end (see page 111). Set up the steamer and steam for three hours at a temperature above 212°F (100°C). It is left to dry.

▶ **21.** View of the finished shawl. Steam setting makes the colors bright and deep.

Lamp Shade

*I*n this exercise demonstrated by Joan Albert Sánchez, we will show you how to make a lamp shade with shantung fabric printed with reserves using the batik method. The reserves are made with small and large bristle brushes to create lines that resemble brushstrokes, giving it a very pictorial appearance. The batik process is applied in four phases: the four reserves with their successive dyes. Once the printing process is finished, we will explain how the lamp shade is mounted on a frame without sewing. Project demonstrated by Miriam Albiñana.

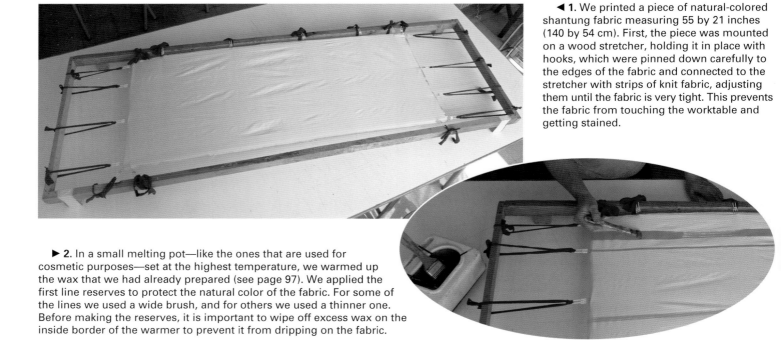

◄ **1.** We printed a piece of natural-colored shantung fabric measuring 55 by 21 inches (140 by 54 cm). First, the piece was mounted on a wood stretcher, holding it in place with hooks, which were pinned down carefully to the edges of the fabric and connected to the stretcher with strips of knit fabric, adjusting them until the fabric is very tight. This prevents the fabric from touching the worktable and getting stained.

► **2.** In a small melting pot—like the ones that are used for cosmetic purposes—set at the highest temperature, we warmed up the wax that we had already prepared (see page 97). We applied the first line reserves to protect the natural color of the fabric. For some of the lines we used a wide brush, and for others we used a thinner one. Before making the reserves, it is important to wipe off excess wax on the inside border of the warmer to prevent it from dripping on the fabric.

▼ **3.** While the wax cooled off we prepared the dye (a reactive dye), following the manufacturer's instructions, in a plastic tub that was large enough for the fabric to fit in. We prepared enough cold water to cover the batik and mixed in a can of light pink color previously dissolved with a small amount of hot water, and approximately 12.5 fluid ounces (375 ml) of vinegar. It was then left to cool.

▼ **4.** The fabric was taken off the stretcher and carefully submerged in the tub. The fabric was stirred for the first ten minutes to prevent the formation of folds, and it was left in the dye for approximately one hour, shaking it gently every once in a while so it dyed evenly. (Use gloves to avoid getting your hands dirty.) Finally, the piece was taken out of the tub and extended flat to dry.

► **5.** Once the piece was completely dry, we proceeded with the second set of reserves, the pink lines. The fabric was mounted on the stretcher again, connecting it at the same points used before to avoid making more holes on the edges of the fabric.

▼ **6.** Different-size brushes were used to make the lines, which were painted in pink along the first reserves, that is, the white ones. Notice that in some cases the brush marks are left on deliberately.

▲ **7.** We prepared a light chestnut-colored dye following the process explained before. The fabric was taken off the stretcher and submerged in the dye mixture, extending flat to dry afterwards.

► **8.** We mounted the fabric on the stretcher again from the same points used before, and we proceeded with the third reserves, in other words, with the ones that covered the areas of color resulting from combining the pink and chestnut areas.

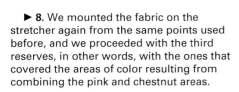

▲ **9.** Next, we did the third dye with violet, following the process used in previous steps.

▲ **10.** Finally, we proceeded with the last set of reserves. Once the fabric was dry, we mounted it again on the stretcher from the same holding points used before, and we applied the reserves that covered the areas of color resulting from combining the three dyes: pink, chestnut, and violet. Here as well, the reserves were made with brushes of various widths.

▲ **11.** The last dye used was dark blue, prepared according to the process explained before. We wrung the fabric with both hands several times to break the wax, to create the characteristic cracked look of this technique.

▶ **12.** The fabric was spread flat for drying. The result is a batik piece with four reserves and five different colors.

13. Before assembling the lamp we needed to remove the wax from the reserves. To do this, the fabric is ironed between two pieces of newspaper. We placed the batik piece between several sheets of paper, having checked first that the dye was set and will not stain the fabric, and we applied heat with a household iron set at the highest temperature level with the steam setting off. The wax melted and was absorbed by the paper. It is important to go over the same areas several times until the wax is completely removed. Then, we removed the papers soaked with wax and replaced them with new ones to continue the process in a different area.

▶ **14.** To assemble the lamp we ordered a frame made of 0.2-inch (5-mm) square iron wire, painted black. It is a 12 by 20 inch (30 cm by 50 cm) square frame with a crosspiece on each side that stands 2.75 inches (7 cm) from the bottom. This is where the lower part of the fabric will be attached. There is also a central cross structure that holds the socket for the lightbulb.

◀ **15.** The batik was mounted on the structure with 0.25-inch (6-mm) wide double-sided tape made especially for framing. This makes the structure strong and durable, and it showcases the screen print since the joints will be concealed because there is no sewing required. With this system the fabric will have clean joints after it is mounted onto the frame. To be able to work comfortably with the structure set on the table, the artist stepped up on a stool. The two-sided tape was applied on the outer side of the wire frame and under the top crosspieces, the ones that form part of the upper side of the shade.

◀ **16.** To begin the assembly, the artist adhered the edge of the fabric onto one of the vertical wires of the frame. After removing the protective backing of the tape, she put it on perfectly aligned and straight, leaving a margin of approximately 0.625 inch (1.5 cm) on the upper part of the fabric to adhere to the upper crosspieces.

◄ **17.** Once the fabric was attached to the front wire, it was connected to the upper crosspiece, removing the backing and aligning it exactly to the outer top part and folding it inwards, forming a hem.

► **18.** The artist continued assembling the shade. The sides and top part of each panel was mounted, making sure that the fabric was perfectly taut. To prevent the fabric from coming undone during the stretching process, the first joint was held in place with pins.

▲ **19.** The joint between the last side and the first end of the fabric was held in place with pins. Next, the excess fabric was trimmed from the upper part, and the joint onto the wire was adjusted. On the corners, the artist made a fold inward to fit it to the angle.

► **20.** Now, the lower part of the fabric was adhered to the inside of the lower crosspieces. To do this, the fabric was cut vertically, just next to the leg, continuing down to the lower crosspiece of the lamp.

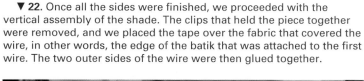

◄ **21.** The fabric from the lower part of each side was connected to the lower crossbars. The protective paper from the adhesive tape was removed and the silk was adhered to the taut wire.

▼ **22.** Once all the sides were finished, we proceeded with the vertical assembly of the shade. The clips that held the piece together were removed, and we placed the tape over the fabric that covered the wire, in other words, the edge of the batik that was attached to the first wire. The two outer sides of the wire were then glued together.

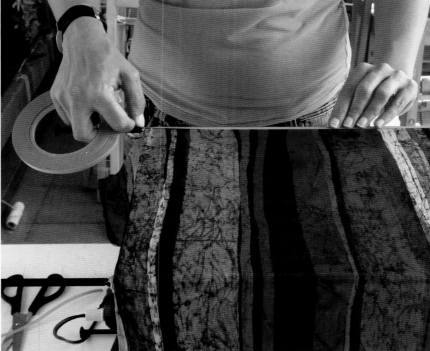

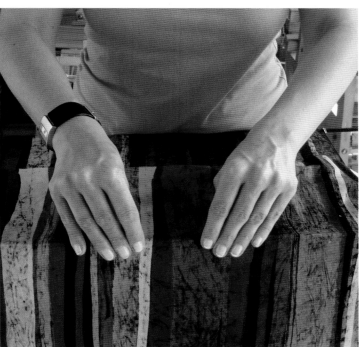

▲ **23.** The fabric was stretched taut and placed over the outer part of the wire, which forms the panel, applying pressure over the tape, from which we removed the protective backing.

► **24.** After placing it past the wire and over the panel, we cut off the excess fabric, leaving a margin of approximately 0.625 inch (1.5 cm).

◀ **25.** Then, we placed the adhesive tape inside the bottom edge, just in the area where it joins the other end of the batik. We removed the protective backing and the fabric was folded over it, forming a hem.

▶ **26.** The hem was connected to the structure (over the fabric) with the tape that was glued to the other side of the wire. This provides a clean and firm joint over one of the wires of the structure. Remember that the cuts and joints must be as straight as possible.

▼ **27.** To finish the assembly, the lower edges of the shade were adjusted. The excess fabric was trimmed off, leaving sufficient margin to be able to connect it to the wire, approximately 0.625 inch (1.5 cm).

▼ **28.** Following the procedure explained before, the fabric was connected to the lower part of each wire.

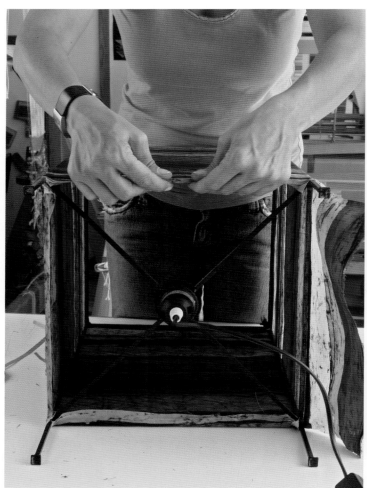

◀ **29.** It was also connected to the other two sides of the wire, located on the inner part of the shade. The joints around the angles were adjusted, that is, the areas where the frame meets the central crossbars.

▼ **30.** The finished lamp with the batik shade.

Personalized Denim Clothing

*O*ne of the many possibilities afforded by textile printing is the personalization of clothing. This way, you can buy articles of clothing already made and adapt them to your own taste by printing different decorative motifs. One of the most interesting approaches is the bleaching of denim fabric, which produces very attractive results. In the following pages, we will demonstrate the process of how to create prints by bleaching clothing made of denim (serge fabric made of white and previously dyed blue cotton fibers) using the screen-printing technique. In this step-by-step guide, developed by Joan Albert Sánchez with the help of Miriam Albiñana, the bleaching process of a double motif is combined with printing with ink, along with other techniques such as the direct painting of some details and the creation of prints on T-shirts that form part of the denim ensemble.

► **1.** In this example we have personalized an ensemble formed by a jacket and a pair of pants for an eight-year-old girl, and several T-shirts with different original designs by Joan Albert Sánchez.

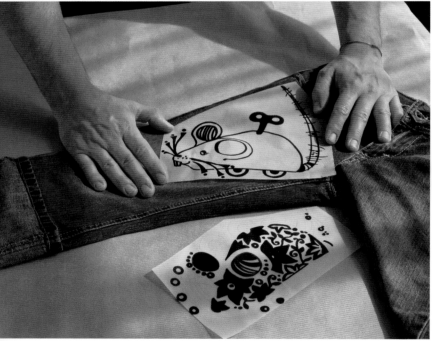

▲ **2.** The main design was printed on the pants with the bleaching technique, and then on a T-shirt using printing ink. There were two motifs: one of them represented the outline of a mouse, and the other represented the body of the same mouse made of floral designs. Once the originals were drawn and transferred to the tracing paper using reprography, they were placed on the clothing to make sure that the motifs fit onto the pieces.

► **3.** We made the screen-printing frame (see page 75), onto which we transferred the designs using photographic emulsion to create the printing matrices. Here, we used a single silk screen for the two motifs, which simplified the process and reduced costs.

▲ **4.** First, we identified the exact location for the main motif by placing both motifs on the pant leg, the same way they would look once the print is done. Here, the little mouse has the tail facing the inside of the leg. The exact placement of the motif with the floral background was marked (which will look like the one below) with pins to make sure that it did not move. This is important because if there are differences between the background motif, which will be done using the discoloration technique, and the outline one, which will be printed with ink, the result will look incoherent.

▲ **5.** Next, we prepared the paste for the bleaching (see page 92), mixing in a plastic or glass container the same amount of pure bleach and water, adding methylcellulose glue slowly, and stirring with a wooden or plastic spoon until the paste became fluid. To place the screen correctly, we took a small amount of bleaching paste with a brush (we recommend utilizing a used brush) and marked the outer dots of the motif.

▲ **6.** The dots, after drying, look white. A newspaper was placed inside the leg where the motif was to be printed. Then, the screen was situated to make a transparency using the previously made white marks as a reference, in such a way that the edges of the background motif (located on the upper part of the screen) coincide with them. We applied a line of paste on the left side of the motif, on the blocked out area of the screen.

◄ **7.** The screen was held firmly in place with one hand to prevent it from moving, while spreading the paste with the other. The paste was extended over the motif with a continuous movement of the squeegee, held at a 45-degree angle and pressing firmly. We went over the motif several times.

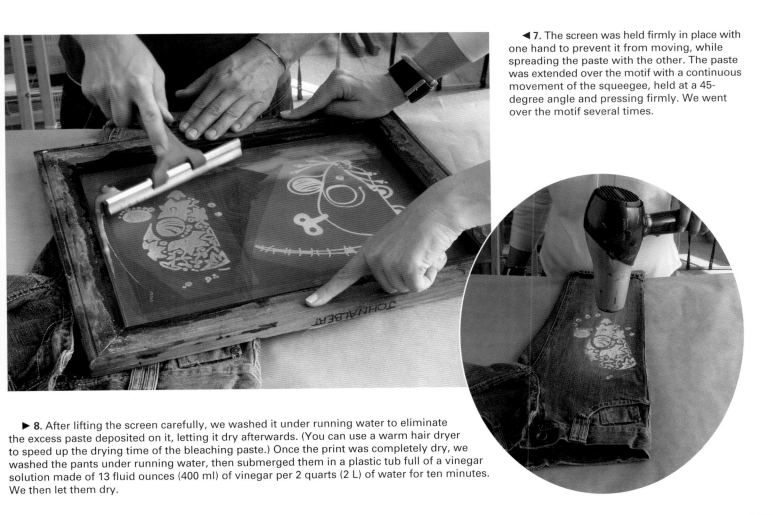

▶ **8.** After lifting the screen carefully, we washed it under running water to eliminate the excess paste deposited on it, letting it dry afterwards. (You can use a warm hair dryer to speed up the drying time of the bleaching paste.) Once the print was completely dry, we washed the pants under running water, then submerged them in a plastic tub full of a vinegar solution made of 13 fluid ounces (400 ml) of vinegar per 2 quarts (2 L) of water for ten minutes. We then let them dry.

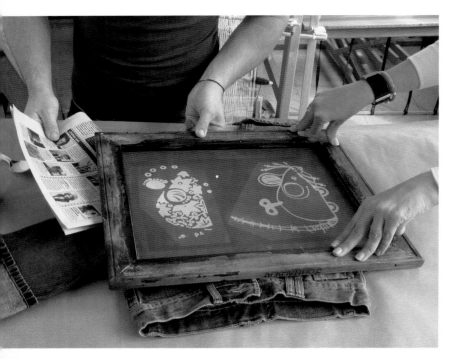

◄ **9.** Next, we proceeded to print the motif of the outline of the mouse. The screen with the motif on the bottom of the screen was placed on the pant leg in such a way that it fit into the previously bleached one. To prevent the other pant leg from getting stained, we protected it by placing a newspaper between the fabric and the screen.

▼ **10.** The motif was printed using dark blue ink. Here as well, the screen was held firmly in place with one hand while working the squeegee with the other.

▲ **11.** The screen was carefully lifted by grabbing one of its corners. The print of the outline matches the bleached background, resulting in a design created with two different colors and techniques. We washed the screen with abundant water and let it dry.

► **12.** To personalize the jacket, we chose cat and mouse designs for the lower area of the sleeves and the neck to match the theme of the pants. We used the bleaching and screen-printing with ink techniques. First, we printed the cat with dark blue ink.

◀ 13. We placed the jacket on the printing table with its back facing up, then placed a piece of lightweight cardboard (plain cardboard or a newspaper would also work) inside the sleeve to prevent the paste from running and staining the other side. We used a screen that has several motifs; therefore, to avoid potential stains we inserted a newspaper between the fabric and the screen, over the areas of the designs that were around the one that was being printed. We printed it as explained before and let it dry.

▼ 14. To personalize the same sleeve, a new screen was used with the design of a winged mouse.

▼ 15. Using the previous print as a reference, we situated the screen in such a way that the winged mouse aligned perfectly with the cat, which is located in front of it.

▶ 16. We printed the motif with bleaching paste. The fabric was previously covered with a newspaper to avoid potential stains (that is, the paste could run and reach the other designs on the screen). A small amount of bleaching paste was applied on the blocked-out side of the screen, placed over the motif, and is spread with a squeegee (here, a plastic applicator was used instead, like the ones used for cosmetic purposes), going over it several times.

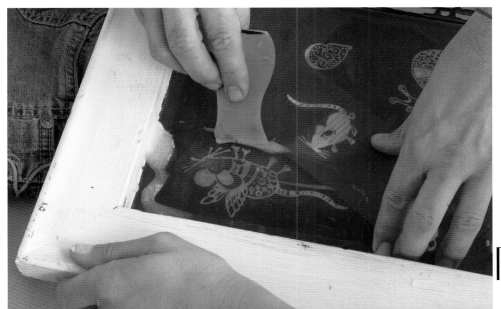

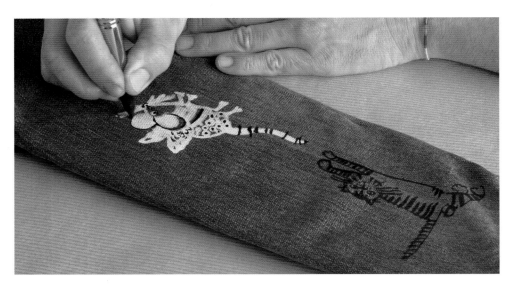

◄ 17. The screen was lifted carefully; then it was washed and left to dry. The bleached print was then dried with a hairdryer. The details on the design were added directly by hand with silk screening ink. With a soft, medium brush we painted the details on the tail, wings, body, ears, and snout, and they were then left to dry. We printed a bleached mouse on the back of the neck and on the other sleeve, completing the details with direct paint as well.

► **18.** To personalize one of the T-shirts to match the denim outfit, we used two different cat designs, while the other T-shirt had the same designs as the pants.

◄ ► **19.** The ensemble consisting of pants, jacket, and two T-shirts finished. Notice the many possibilities available by combining designs using the silk-screening technique. The main motif printed on the pants with bleaching and blue ink has been printed also on the orange T-shirt using two different colors.

Curtain with Devoré

*I*n this project, designed by Joan Albert Sánchez, we demonstrate the complete process for creating a velvet curtain. The work involves two different techniques: the first step will be carried out with the devoré technique, and the second will consist of dyeing the curtain. The result is a decorative curtain, very appropriate for the window treatment of an interior decorated with a combination of styles with a vintage or retro flavor, which is also the style of this curtain.

▶ **1.** For this project we started with a screen based on the original design by Elisa Rubió (see page 75), inspired on the free forms that were in style during the 1950s and 1960s.

▼ **2.** For the curtain itself we chose a 55 by 39 inch (140 by 100 cm) length of velvet fabric with a silk base (a protein fiber) and rayon pile (regenerated cellulose fibers).

▶ **3.** The first step consisted of preparing the devoré paste according to the manufacturer's instructions. In a graduated plastic or glass container we combined 5.75 fluid ounces (170 ml) of devoré paste with 1 fluid ounce (30 ml) of reactive, mixing them together with a wooden stick (plastic or glass would also work) until they are completely dissolved. This preparation should be made in a very well-ventilated area; use gloves to protect the skin in case it comes in contact with the paste.

◄ **4.** We placed the fabric on the printing table over kraft paper with the under side facing up, that is, with the pile side touching the paper, and held it in place with pins to prevent it from moving. Next, we placed the screen over the fabric in the desired position and dispensed a line of paste on one of the sides of the motif, on the blocked-out area.

▲ **5.** We held the screen firmly with one hand to prevent it from moving, and with the other hand we spread the devoré paste with a squeegee held at a 45-degree angle, making several passes to make sure that the product penetrated the fabric.

◄ **6.** We continued printing the motif, moving the screen in such a way that the new motif did not touch the one printed before. Once the print was completed, we removed the frame, holding it from both sides and lifting it carefully to prevent the paste from touching the skin and from dripping on the fabric.

► **7.** We continued printing new motifs over the length of the fabric, placing some of them topside up and others topside down. Although there is no guiding pattern for the arrangement of the designs, it is important for the composition to be evenly distributed.

◄ **8.** Since we were looking for a free and loose composition, we printed only half of the motif in some areas of the sides of the fabric.

► **9.** We were true to the rhythm of the composition, which will end up with half of the motif printed on the fabric and the other half on the kraft paper.

► **10.** We continued printing until the fabric was covered, then let it dry.

► **11.** One of the advantages of the silk-screening technique is that you can use old designs or parts of them to make new prints. In this case, we used the adaptation of an old, complex design to complement the main motif. To do this, we covered the rest of the motif on both sides of the screens with contact paper, leaving the two central circles uncovered, which is the design that we will print.

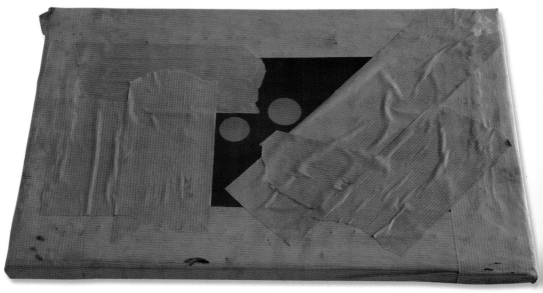

12. We proceeded to print the two circles in the areas of the fabric located between the main designs, avoiding touching the motifs that were still wet with the frame of the screen.

▼ 13. In areas that were very narrow or located very close to the main motifs, we only printed a single circle. To protect the fabric we placed a newspaper under the screen, below the circle that is not going to be printed.

◄ 14. Once dry, the fabric was placed on the worktable over a clean cloth and ironed with the underside facing up, with a piece of fabric between the latter and the iron. We set the iron at the lowest heat setting, increasing it if needed, but without the steam. The look of the devoré must be checked constantly until it becomes light brown (see page 90), because if the temperature gets warmer the fabric can burn. This procedure should be carried out in a very well-ventilated area.

► 15. We washed the fabric to dislodge the viscose fibers, gently rubbing it in abundant water. The fabric's silk base was visible through the motif. We wrung the fabric gently and kept it wet in a plastic tub.

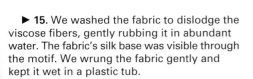

◄ 16. Then, we proceeded with the second phase of the project. We chose the colors based on the design, inspired by color combinations of the 1950s and 1960s. We prepared the materials (from the H. Dupont brand): a chestnut-brown selective dye for celluloid fibers; a deep-blue selective dye for protein fibers; fixative; salt, which works as a dye fixative on viscose; and vinegar, which works as a fixative for silk.

TABLE OF DOSES FOR DEVORÉ DYEING*

Weight of the fabric	Type of Devoré		Dose
From 0.4 to 0.9 oz (10 to 25 g) of dry fabric	Light devoré: it has 70 percent celluloid fibers (viscose, for example) and 30 percent protein fibers (silk, for example)	2 tsp (10 ml) of dye for celluloid fibers	2 cups (0.5 L) of water, 3 drops of vinegar, and 1 tsp (5 ml) of salt
		1 tsp (5 ml) of dye for protein fibers	
		6 drops of fixative	
	Very deep devoré: 50 percent celluloid fibers and 50 percent protein fibers.	1.5 tsp (7 ml) of dye for celluloid fibers	
		1.5 tsp (7 ml) of dye for protein fibers	
		3 drops of fixative	
From 0.8 to 1.3 oz (24 to 36 g) of dry fabric	Light devoré: 70 percent celluloid fibers and 30 percent protein fibers	4 tsp (20 ml) of dye for celluloid fibers	4 cups (1 L) of water, 6 drops of vinegar, and 2 tsp (10 ml) of salt
		2 tsp (10 ml) of dye for protein fibers	
		12 drops of fixative	
	Very deep devoré: 50 percent celluloid fibers and 50 percent protein fibers.	3 tsp (14 ml) of dye for celluloid fibers	
		3 tsp (14 ml) of dye for protein fibers	
		6 drops of fixative	
From 1.2 to 1.8 oz (35 to 50 g) of dry fabric	Light devoré: 70 percent celluloid fibers and 30 percent protein fibers	6 tsp (30 ml) of dye for celluloid fibers	6 cups (1.5 L) of water, 9 drops of vinegar, and 3 tsp (15 ml) of salt
		3 tsp (15 ml) of dye for protein fibers	
		18 drops of fixative	
	Very deep devoré: 50 percent celluloid fibers and 50 percent protein fibers.	4 tsp (21 ml) of dye for synthetic fabrics	
		4 tsp (21 ml) of dye for protein fibers	
		9 drops of fixative	
From 1.8 to 2.5 oz (50 to 70 g) of dry fabric	Light devoré: 70 percent celluloid fibers and 30 percent protein fibers	8 tsp (40 ml) of dye for celluloid fibers	8.5 cups (2 L) of water, 12 drops of vinegar, and 4 tsp (20 ml) of salt
		4 tsp (20 ml) of dye for protein fibers	
		24 drops of fixative	
	Very deep devoré: 50 percent celluloid fibers and 50 percent protein fibers.	6 tsp (28 ml) of dye for celluloid fibers	
		6 tsp (28 ml) of dye for protein fibers	
		12 drops of fixative	
From 2.8 to 3.5 oz (80 to 100 g) of dry fabric	Light devoré: 70 percent celluloid fibers and 30 percent protein fibers	12 tsp (60 ml) of dye for celluloid fibers	12.5 cups (3 L) of water, 15 drops of vinegar, and 6 tsp (30 ml) of salt
		6 tsp (30 ml) of dye for protein fibers	
		36 drops of fixative	
	Very deep devoré: 50 percent celluloid fibers and 50 percent protein fibers.	8.5 tsp (42 ml) of dye for celluloid fibers	
		8.5 tsp (42 ml) of dye for protein fibers	
		18 drops of fixative	

* Table adapted from the technical instructions of the brand-name dye Alter Ego, produced by H. Dupont, which is used in these exercises.

To prepare the dye we recommend the use of decalcified water or distilled water. We also recommend the use of white vinegar. The volume of salt should be measured with a graduated measuring cup.

Before dyeing the fabric, it is a good idea to do several tests on scrap pieces of the same fabric and with the same devoré to make sure that the concentration of dye is correct and withstands washing appropriately; in other words, make sure that it is suitable for the desired technique.

◄ 17. We prepared 8.5 cups (2 L) of water (preferably decalcified or distilled) in a container and heated it until it was warm. Then, we transferred it to a different container that was large and fire-resistant and had a wide opening (for example, a large pot). We added 12 drops of vinegar and twenty-four of fixative with a dropper. With a measuring cup we prepared 4 tsp (20 ml) of salt and added it to the water as well. Next, we measured 8 tsp (40 ml) of brown dye and 4 tsp (20 ml) of blue.

▲ 18. We added the colors to the mixture and stirred with a wooden tool (metal or glass would also work) until the liquid looked thoroughly blended.

◄ 19. We carefully submerged the wet fabric in the selective dye, trying to avoid any folds.

► 20. We stirred it for five minutes with the wooden stick, pulling it out several times to avoid the formation of folds. The fabric appeared with the two colors: brown for the viscose fibers and blue for the silk fibers.

◄ 21. Next, the pot was heated on the stove set at low temperature and the fabric was stirred for five minutes to evenly distribute the dye. The temperature was increased to maximum and left on the stove until it boiled (about twenty minutes, although the time depends on the amount of dye and type of water), stirring once in a while. Once it began to boil, we turned off the stove and let it rest for ten minutes.

▼ 22. The fabric was removed carefully, since it was still hot; you can use wood tongs if necessary to transfer it to the sink for washing. We rinsed it under cold running water.

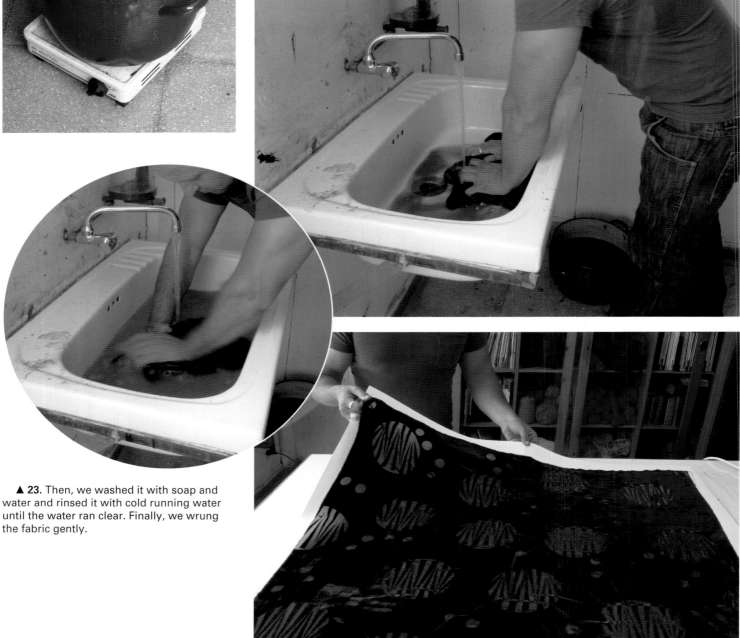

▲ 23. Then, we washed it with soap and water and rinsed it with cold running water until the water ran clear. Finally, we wrung the fabric gently.

► 24. We extended the fabric on a sheet of blotting paper spreading it flat on the work surface with the pile side facing up. It was left to dry until it felt damp to the touch.

▲ **25.** To finish, we placed the fabric on a sheet of blotting paper and ironed it on the backside while still wet, placing a piece of blotting paper over it to fix the dye.

▶ **26.** The curtain finished and hung. The devoré design is visible on the blue of the silk fibers, which adds transparency and contrast against the opaque brown surface whose velvet pile creates light brown reflections.

Armchair Decorated with Gutta

*I*n this final step-by-step exercise we will explain how to decorate an armchair with water-based gutta. Here, the gutta is applied directly to the design, which differs from the normal application in the serti process, where it is used specifically to create outline reserves to define the outlines of the motifs (see page 104). Therefore, this project, developed by Elisa Rubió, is an excellent example of one of the many possibilities offered by the use of gutta in direct printing, that is, through the direct application on the fabric. This technique can be used to create prints on any type of fabric and fibers, especially on clothing, upholstery and pillows, and handbags. As usual, the possibilities are only limited by your own creativity.

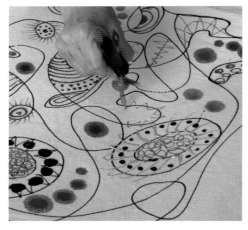

◄ **1.** We created a print to upholster a store-bought chair. This chair is factory-made and comes with a natural-color taffeta cover made of thick cotton thread, measuring 30.75 by 31.50 by 28.75 inches (78 by 80 by 72 cm). The legs are made of beech wood and it has a seat with a removable cover.

► **2.** Before we began the project it was necessary to plan the design by making a test. We mounted a piece of fabric that was similar to the upholstery of the chair on a fixed frame. First, we drew the overall background design with black gutta using curved intersecting lines. Then, we defined the details of the print with gutta of different colors: zigzag lines, circles and dots, among others.

▲ **3.** We continued creating the motifs that were to be used on the upholstery later, testing different color combinations and various decorative motifs over the undulating background design.

► **4.** The results helped establish the resources that were to be used on the print: black undulating lines and details in color and metallic gutta, with predominance of zigzag, undulating, and circle designs. It also helped rule out certain colors. This test is used as a guide throughout the entire printing process.

▲ **5.** We began the print by drawing the design on the back of the chair with black gutta, creating a background of intersecting curving lines. We also created a few circular designs that were to be filled with color gutta later on. The gutta was applied directly from the tube, which was fitted with a wide tip, perfect for drawing the lines.

▲ **6.** To emphasize the painterly aspect of the design, we made some lines thicker than others. We proceeded in an orderly fashion, letting the gutta dry completely before moving on to the next phase, or placing the chair in a different position during the process to avoid staining.

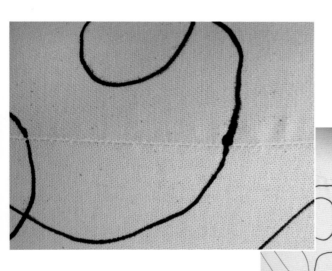

◄ **7.** The joints or the seams of the upholstery become critical areas because their slight protrusion makes it difficult for the applicator to slide easily, which can create stains. To avoid this, we moved the applicator carefully (see the line on the left of the picture), or we stopped when we reached a seam and resumed on the other side of it (see the line on the right side of the picture).

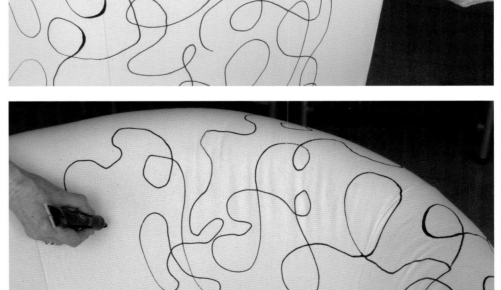

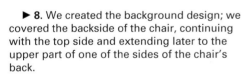

► **8.** We created the background design; we covered the backside of the chair, continuing with the top side and extending later to the upper part of one of the sides of the chair's back.

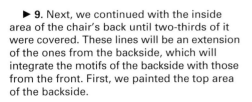

► **9.** Next, we continued with the inside area of the chair's back until two-thirds of it were covered. These lines will be an extension of the ones from the backside, which will integrate the motifs of the backside with those from the front. First, we painted the top area of the backside.

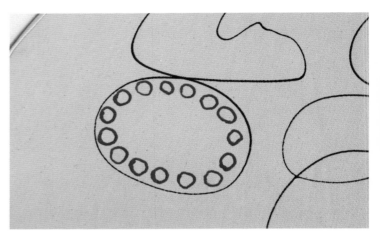

◀ 10. Then, we painted the lower part of the chair's back, extending the lines to the back and front of the chair's cushion. We extended the lower line of the chair's back, located in the background, onto the surface of the cushion where we applied the design, which covered two-thirds of the upholstery and continued until it reached the chair's back again (line on the foreground).

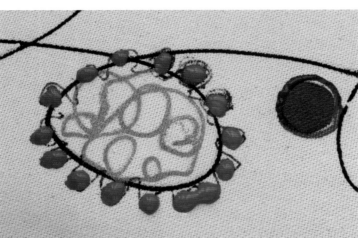

▲ 11. Once the background motif was finished and completely dry, we painted the decorative motifs with colored gutta. We decorated the cushion first. In some of the circular motifs, where lines intersect, we drew circles.

◀ 12. Others were filled with wiggly metallic lines made with copper-colored gutta and decorated on the outside with zigzag lines and different colored dots. The design is complemented with colored circles.

▶ **13.** We continued decorating the cushion with red, orange, blue, and metallic gutta. We placed a metal applicator over the tube's tip to make copper lines thinner than the different colored ones.

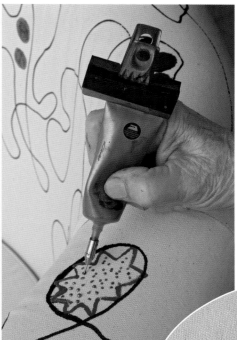

◄◄ **14.** Then, we proceeded with the decorations on the chair's back using the same design shapes used before on the cushion. We painted different colored circles, applying the gutta directly from the tube.

◄ **15.** We created star-shaped designs inside the ringlet on the background motifs, and we filled in the star with a series of dots.

▼ **16.** Other ringlets were decorated with small copper-colored lines, as if they were sun's rays.

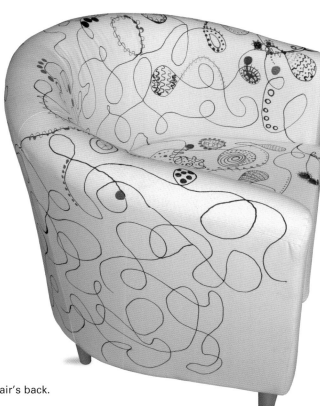

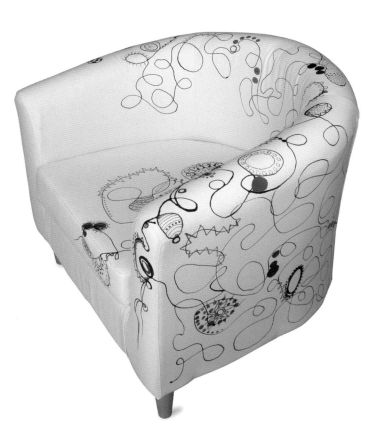

▲ **17.** We continued decorating the top and outer sides of the chair's back. In the areas where there were several layered colors or forms, we let the gutta dry completely before the next color was applied.

▶ **18.** We also worked in the area inside the chair's back.

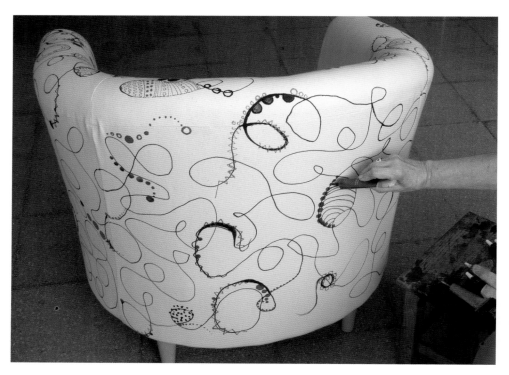

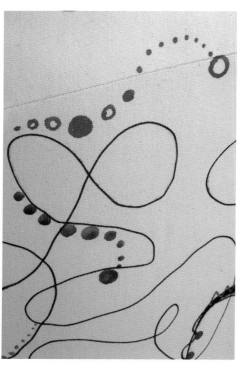

▲ **19.** We continued printing the backside of the chair, the outer side of the chair's back, with different colored gutta. The printing was applied in an orderly manner, from left to right, and in the direction in which the design of the back was printed. The inside of some of the rings were decorated with undulating or curved lines, similar to the designs used in other parts of the chair.

▲ **20.** Paint a motif based on the repetition of circular elements to create a wavy border.

◄ **21.** The lines were combined with copper-colored elements.

► **22.** Finally, the motif of the left front area of the chair was applied, which balances out the overall composition of the project. First, we made the central motif with copper-colored gutta, forming a zigzag design with an inscribed green spiral; we finished with orange and black details. Next, we drew a black, curved line that spanned along the chair's skirt and extended up the front of the arm.

▲ **23.** Once dry, the design was finished with green, red, and blue gutta and was left to dry.

◄ **24.** The finished chair.

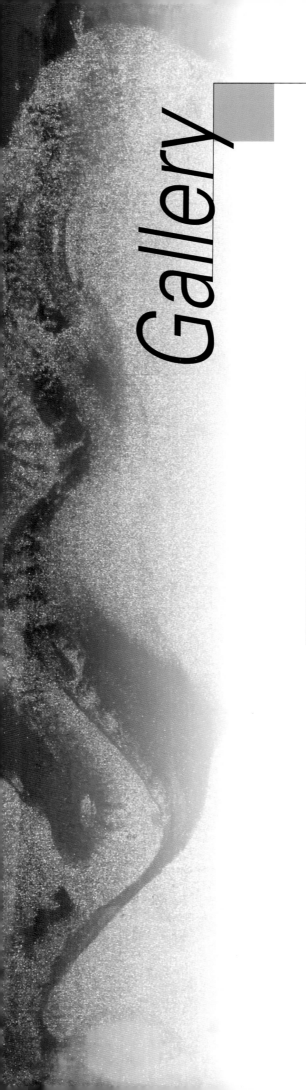

► Lourdes Perelló and Julia Rodríguez. *Dancing,* 2006. Painting done in serti on silk by Lourdes Perelló, and lead glass with the Tiffany technique by Julia Rodríguez. 7 7/8 × 6 1/4 inches (20 × 16 cm).

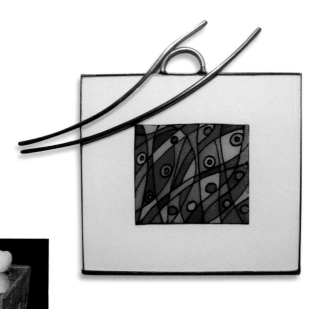

◄ Deseda+.Table, serti on silk over a metal structure lighted from the inside, and glass cover, 2006.

▲ Montserrat Torras i Lladó. Doll, serti on silk with interior cotton lining reinforcement and synthetic filler, 2004. 11 7/8 × 6 1/4 inches (30 × 15 cm).

◄ Pepa de Funes. Scarves (detail), batik on silk, 2006, 78 3/4 × 35 1/2 inches (200 × 90 cm) each.

► Elisa Farrús. Handbag, *"Print-temps"* collection, 2006. Dyed, stenciled, and cotton, painted directly. 11 7/8 × 11 7/8 inches (30 × 30 cm).

◄▼ Marian Piano. *El abrigo de tus sueños* (The coat of your dreams), 2007. Coat that can turn into a pillow. Silkscreen lining on cotton. 17 3/4 × 25 1/4 inches (45 × 64 cm), approximately.

▼ Lourdes Perelló and Genoveva Peralta. *Girablau,* 2005–2006. Fan with devoré and painted velvet fabric, with bocapi wood ribs, assembled by hand.

155

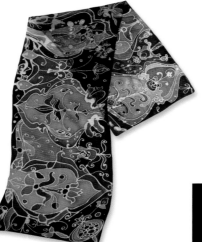

► Cet Xalest Disseny. Duvet cover for a twin bed, pillow, and bedding sham made of screen-printed cotton. Original design and limited production created by the school-shop Xalest, special work center for persons with physical and other disabilities.

▲ Rosa Bascón. Scarf, batik on silk, 2007. 51 × 11 7/8 inches (130 × 30 cm).

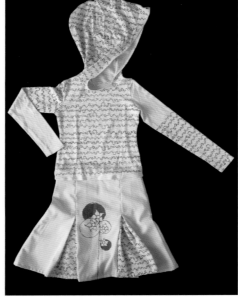

► Lidia Azuara. Screen-printed pleated skirt lined with cotton serge inside the pleats, and cotton jersey top. Collection "Ella en el espejo," 2006. Skirt: 20 × 31 1/2 inches (51 × 80 cm); top: 35 × 55 inches (89 × 140 cm).

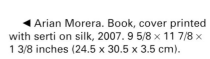

▲ Nadia Faus. Gloves, screen-printed lycra, 2007. 9 × 3 1/8 inches (23 × 8 cm).

◄ Arian Morera. Book, cover printed with serti on silk, 2007. 9 5/8 × 11 7/8 × 1 3/8 inches (24.5 x 30.5 x 3.5 cm).

◀▲ Francisco Pérez-Dolz. Shawl, batik on silk, circa 1933-1934. 59 x 25 1/2 inches (150 x 65 cm).

▼ Carles de Rosselló. Dress, georgette crepe on silk printed with blocks, 1992. Photograph by Colita.

▲ Teresa Lladó. Hamper printed with bamboo stems cut in half, bamboo trunks, and banana fruit, finished with a hem at the bottom made of napa leather, wood structure, 2007. 23 5/8 × 13 3/4 × 13 3/4 inches (60 × 35 × 35 cm).

◀ Dolores Noguer. *Vestit Matisse,* 2002. Dress made of dyed devoré velvet and silk chiffon with Swarovski crystal appliqués. Size 4 (European 38). Made by Llorens Pons. Photograph by Marc Guillén.

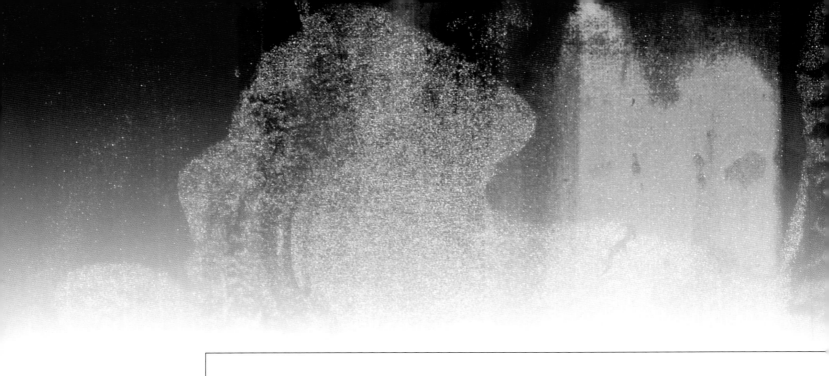

Glossary

b

Baque. This is a recipient for the ink or paint that will be applied to the block in the hand-stamping technique with wood blocks.

Batik. This technique consists of creating reserves on the fabric by applying melted wax, and then applying colored dyes when the wax has cooled. The layer of wax, which can be applied with a tjanting, brush, palette knife, or blocks, protects the fabric and preserves the original underlying color. Batik works have a characteristic cracking that results from the cracking of the wax reserve.

Bleaching. This technical process is based on modifying the original colors of the fabric with chemicals. It consists of printing an impression with an agent that causes the fibers to lose their color and acquire a tone or color that is different from the original.

Block. This is the stamp that is used for printing the desired shape on the textile. Blocks can be made of wood, metal, or linoleum, although it is possible to use any number of common materials and vegetable elements for making impressions.

c

Canting Tool. Also known as a tjanting, this is used for making wax reserves in batik. It consists of a wood handle with a small metal container at one end, which has one or more needle spouts.

d

Design motif. A motif consisting of one or several shapes printed in a specific pattern on the textile.

Devoré. This printing technique affects the texture of the fabric and creates areas where part of it is eliminated with chemical agents, leaving the base of the textile uncovered. It consists of printing an impression with a caustic chemical, which dries and then in the presence of heat will destroy certain fibers of the fabric and leave others intact.

Dyes. These are substances used for permanently coloring textiles. The process requires the textiles to be submerged in a bath, where they are penetrated by the dyes, and after fixing they form a chemical union with the components of the fibers.

g

Gutta. Also known as gutta percha, this is the sap of various species of trees that grow in Southeast Asia. After proper refining and preparation, it is used in the serti technique for creating reserves and outlining shapes to control the flow of paint and separate painted areas. It can also be used by printing directly, for outlining and decorating motifs that were previously stamped or painted directly on the fabric.

i

Impression. This refers to transferring a design by using pressure, printing or stamping it on the fabric.

m

Motif. The base of a repeated design in a printed textile; in other words, it is the basic unit of the design that is extended in all directions on the fabric.

p

Paint. This is a paste with a fluid consistency composed of one or several pigments mixed with an agglutinate. There are paints for textiles and specific paints for silk. The latter are often referred to as dyes.

Pattern. A printed piece in which the motif extends across the entire textile, repeating itself according to a determined sequence.

Printing Ink. Acrylic paste with pigments in water, and in some cases other products that give them special properties. With a creamy consistency, they are semifluid and are used for printing with blocks and in serigraphy.

r

Reserve. The part of the textile that is protected by the application of specific materials, which keeps it from being colored by the dyes or paints that color the rest of the fabric.

s

Satin. This is a textile formed by the weave passing over the warp and vice versa, with the minimum number of separate and equidistant crossing threads and with some floats or missed crossings, resulting in a smooth surface with a glossy look.

Screen. This is a support consisting of a frame with a tightly stretched screen that is used for serigraphy or silk screen printing.

Serigraphy. This is also known as silk screen printing. It is a printing technique in which the image is created by forcing ink through a fine fabric screen, which is in contact with a textile, with a squeegee. The ink only passes through the open areas and stays on the screen in the closed ones, creating a printed design on the textile.

Serti. A French term for a technique of printing on silk that uses reserves, usually gutta, to outline and contain the area where the paint will be applied.

Stamp. This word derives from the Germanic *estampon*, which translates to "grind" or "print," and also means to create a form. Giving form with the use of a block or a plate.

Steam Setting. This is a technique for fixing silk dyes with an alcohol base by applying steam.

Stitch. This is a weave formed by a crisscross screen. It can be made of single threads that cross each other, or warped fabrics.

Subtractive Method of Color. This refers to the method through which colors combine, that is, all the pastes and colorants that are used in printing. There are three fundamental, or primary, colors: magenta, cyan, and yellow. These are the basic colors, which are mixed to create all the other colors. At the same time, the primary colors cannot be created from the other colors, and black results from mixing the three primaries. Mixing the primaries creates the secondary colors, and mixing a secondary with a primary creates a tertiary color. All colors have their complement; they are a secondary color and the primary color that was not used in the mixture of that secondary.

t

Taffeta. This is a fabric where each thread of the warp crosses a thread of the weft, over and under. This is the simplest weave.

Tjanting. A Javanese word for the needle spout that is used for creating reserves in batik.

Twill. Textiles in which the crossing of the weft threads move a space to the side with each crossing of the warp, which results in a diagonal "pattern." It is easily identified since the lines on the surface are at a 45-degree angle.

Bibliography
and Acknowledgments

GILLOW, J., SENTANCE, B. *World Textures.* Thames & Hudson. London, England, 2005.
MORGADES, C. *Silk Painting for Beginners.* h.f.ullman. Potsdam, Germany, 2008.
MOYER, S.L. *Silk Painting for Fashion and Fine Art.* Watson-Guptill. New York, NY, 1995.
NIETO GALÁN, A. *Colouring Textiles.* Springer. New York, NY, 2001.
WELLS, K. *Fabric Dyeing and Printing.* Conran Octopus. London, England, 2000.

The authors wish to thank:

Parramon Editions and especially María Fernanda Canal for her support and for trusting us to carry out this project. We also thank Joan Soto, Sergi Oriola, and the entire team at Nos & Soto for their help and good work.

To the collaborating institutions:

*Escola Superior de Disseny i d'Art Llotja
Ciutat de Balaguer, 12. 08022 Barcelona
www.llotja.cat*

*Departament d'Estampació
i Tintatges Artístics, Llotja
Ciutat Balaguer, 12. 08022 Barcelona
estampaciotextil@hotmail.com*

*Museu de l'Estampació Textil
de Premiá de Mar
Joan XXIII, 2-8. 08330 Premiá de Mar
www.museuestampaciopremiademar.org*

*Centre de Documentació
iMuseu Textil de Terrassa
Salmerón, 25. 08222 Terrassa
www.cdmt.es*

*Arxiu Històric de la Ciutat,
Institut de Cultura de Barcelona
C/ de Santa Llúcia, 1. 08002 Barcelona
www.bcn.cat/icub*

*Associació d'Estudis Científics i Culturals,
Premiá de Mar
Camí Ral, 54. 08330 Premiá de Mar
www.aeccweb.org*

*Atelier Mendini, Milan
Via Sannio, 24. 20137 Milano
www.ateliermendini.it*

To the people and the professionals who have unselfishly given us their help:

*Teresa Bastardes
Juan María Medina Ayllón
Enric Pardo de Campos
Esther de Prados
Carme, Francesc and M. Pilar Pérez-Dolz*

To these companies for their generous help:

*SODINTEX
Diputación, 237. 08007 Barcelona
www.sodintex.com*

*MARBAY S.L.
Vial Mogent, 10. 08170 Montornés del Vallés
www.marbay.es*

*CASA RIGOL. BELLES ARTS
Consell de Cent 264. 08011 Barcelona
www.rigolbellesarts.com*

To the artists who have collaborated:

*Adaia Anglés: adaia42@hotmail.com
Lidia Azuara: www.lidiaazuara.com
Montserrat Coloma: montsiponsi@gmail.com
Deseda+: www.desedamas.com
Rosa M. Bascón: rosabascon@yahoo.es
Elisa Farrús: http://textilartelise.com
Nadia Faus: nadiafaus@hotmail.com
Pepa de Funes
Teresa Lladó: www.mtersallado.net
Rosa María Martín Sol: www.2punts.com
Aina Mas Flaquer: aynabcn@hotmail.com
Laura Meseguer: www.laurameseguer.com
Arian Morera: arianmorera@terra.es
Laura Muniesa: lauramuniesa@hotmail.com
Dolors Noguer: www.dolorsnoguer.com
Genoveva Peralta: genep@ya.com
Lourdes Perelló: pinzellades@hotmail.com
Carme Pérez-Dolz: carmenperezdolz@tinet.org
Monica Pérez Sierra: Bugambilia: bugambilia@hotmail.com
Marian Piano: missmarian14@hotmail.com
Carlota Racionero: chorly3@hotmail.com
Maria Rives: malena2021@hotmail.com
Queralt Rota: quer_alt81@hotmail.com
Maria Roca: www.mariaroca.com
Julia Rodríguez. Vitraloi: vitraloi@telefonica.net
Carles de Roselló: carlesder@telefonica.net
Llibertat Tomás y Raul Muñoz: llibertatomas@hotmail.com
Montserrat Torras i Lladó: montsetll@gmail.com
Mónica Usón
Cet Xalest Disseny: xalest@terra.es*

Without whom this book would not have been possible.

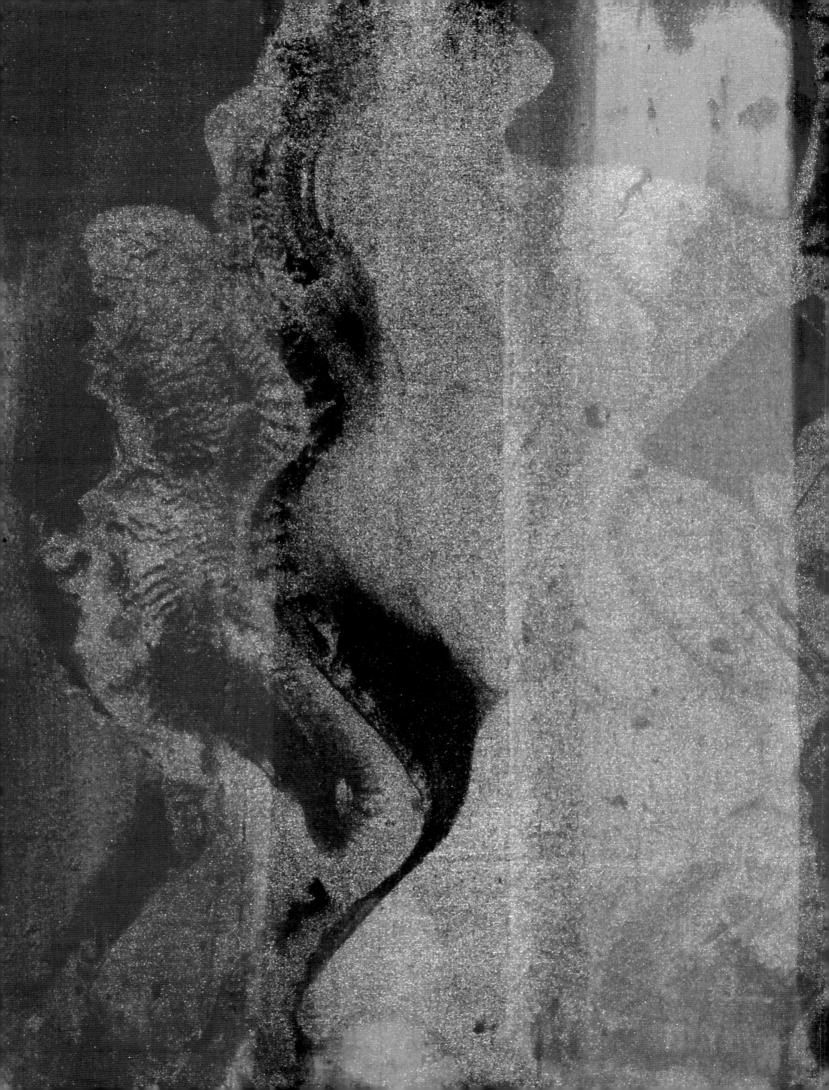